VIOLETS
of the
United States

Also by the Author
Rock Garden Plants
Gentians for Your Garden
Primroses and Spring

VIOLETS
of the
United States

Doretta Klaber

South Brunswick and New York: A. S. Barnes and Company
Rutherford, Madison and Teaneck: Fairleigh Dickinson University Press
London: Thomas Yoseloff Ltd

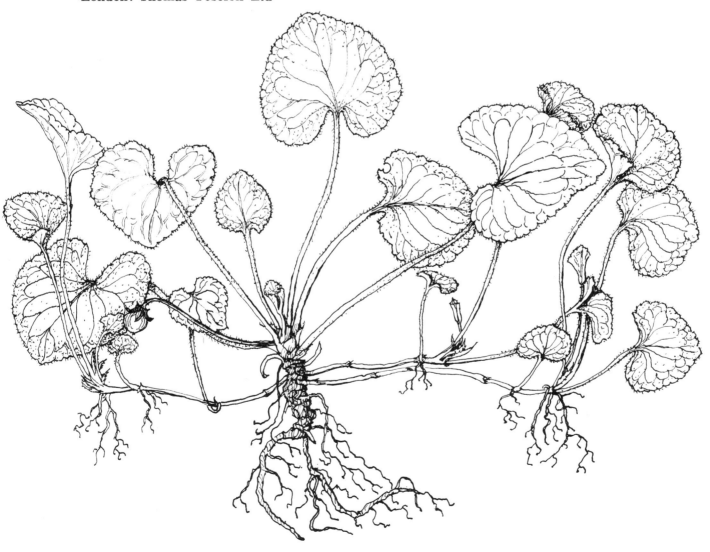

A. S. Barnes & Co., Inc.
Cranbury, New Jersey 08512

Associated University Presses, Inc.
Cranbury, New Jersey 08512

Thomas Yoseloff Ltd
108 New Bond Street
London W1Y OQX, England

Library of Congress Cataloging in Publication Data

Klaber, Doretta.
    Violets of the United States.

    Bibliography: p.
    Includes index.
    1. Violets—United States—Identification. I. Title.
QK495.V5K56   583'.135'0973   77-75038
ISBN 0-498-07394-7 (Barnes)
ISBN 0-8386-7915-3 (FDUP)

Printed in the United States of America

To Dr. Norman H. Russell
only he and I
know
how much I owe to him, and

In memory of my good companion
for 58 years
Eugene Henry Klaber

Authors of Botanical Names

Ait. = William Aiton 1731–1793
Baker = John Gilbert Baker 1834–1920
Benth. = George Bentham 1800–1884
Brainerd = Ezra Brainerd 1844–1924
Degener = Otto Degener 1899–
Don. G. = George Don 1798–1856
Dougl. = David Douglas 1799–1834
Ell. = Stephen Elliott 1771–1830
Geyer = Earl A. Geyer 1809–1853
Ging. = Baron Frederic C. J. Gingins de Lassaraz 1790–ca. 1843
Gray = Asa Gray 1810–1888
Greene = Edward L. Greene 1842–1915
Harper = Roland M. Harper 1878–1967
Henry = Leroy K. Henry 1905–
Hook. = William Jackson Hooker 1785–1865
House = Homer D. House 1878–1949
Howell = Thomas Howell 1842–1912
Kell. = Albert Kellogg 1813–1887
L. = Linnaeus [Carl von Linné] 1707–1778
Le Conte = John Eaton Le Conte 1784–1860
Ledeb. = Karl Friedrich von Ledebour 1785–1851
Lloyd = Francis Ernest Lloyd 1868–1947
Michx. = André Michaux 1746–1802
Nelson = Aven Nelson 1859–ca. 1945
Nutt. = Thomas Nuttall 1786–1859
Piper = Charles V. Piper 1867–1926
Pollard = Charles L. Pollard 1872–1945
Pursh = Frederick T. Pursh 1774–1820
Reichenb. = Henry Gottlieb Ludwig Reichenbach 1793–1879
Russell = Norman H. Russell 1921–
Rydb. = Per Axel Rydberg 1860–1931
Schrank = Franz P. Schrank 1747–1835
Schwein. = Lewis David von Schweinitz 1780–1834
J. E. Smith = James Edward Smith 1759–1828
Steud. = Ernst G. Steudel 1783–1856
Torr. = John Torrey 1796–1873
Walt. = Thomas Walter ca. 1740–1788
Wats. = Sereno Watson 1826–1892
Wherry = Edgar T. Wherry 1885–
Willd. = Karl Ludwig Willdenow 1765–1812

CONTENTS

FOREWORD

In 1817, more than 150 years ago, J. E. Smith stated in the Cyclopaedia of Abraham Rees, "The poetry, the romance, the scenery, of every country, is embroidered with the violet, from Caledonia to Aracadia. . . .", and further, ". . . . a full scientific botanical essay on Viola might display as much skill and learning, and be made subservient to as much philosophical illustration of botany, as any monographical subject that could be chosen."

Doretta Klaber has prepared for us, with most arduous labor, with deep intuition, and with most marvelous skill and enthusiasm, both a work of art and a genuine scientific production. I believe that her drawings are entirely without equal in botanical works for their clarity, exactness, and artistic quality. Furthermore, though she has sought my aid and the aid of other taxonomic specialists in making her decisions, and in supplementing her own acute observations on violets in nature and in her garden, she has used her own judgment and intuition in the classification of the genus in the United States. In several years of correspondence with her, she has seen and told me many things about the violets that I had not learned in 20 years of research on them.

To J. E. Smith, if he is listening in the Garden of God, where he walks now, this book will speak the fulfillment of his prediction. And to those who read its learned and delightful statements, to those who look at these magnificent drawings of the very real beauties of nature, this book will speak pleasure and knowledge. Like the lovely plants it describes, it will speak an awareness and a reverence for the forms of life. And it will speak spring. For the season of spring belongs to the violets.

NORMAN H. RUSSELL
Central State University
Edmond, Oklahoma 73034

ACKNOWLEDGMENTS

This book could not have been produced without the cooperation of the many who have collected or shared plants and sent them to me, often with descriptions, slides, photographs, and other pertinent information. Whether they were nurserymen or gardeners, professional botanists or amateurs, all took an interest far beyond the call of business or friendship, and many were strangers who helped because of their love of violets or their interest in the project. These donors are:

From the far west:

Alaska—Christine Heller, Aline Strutz, Helen White

Washington—University of Washington herbarium sheets, Rosina Laughlin, George Schenk, Charles Thurman, Virginia Winegar

Oregon—Florence Bellis, Siskiyou Nursery, Virginia Winegar

California—Jean Ireland, Dorothy K. Young

From the western mountain states:

Colorado—Mary Ann Heacock

Montana—State University, W. E. Booth, Hilda Kraus

Wyoming—Virginia Thomas

From the north central states:

Michigan—Tillie Bernhard

Minnesota—University of Minnesota, Paul H. Munson, Clair Phillips

Missouri—Missouri Botanical Garden Herbarium Sheets, Ruth Mooney

Ohio—Harry W. Butler

South Dakota—Claude A. Barr

From the southwest:

Texas—Janice B. Lacey

From the south:

Florida—Dorcas Brigham, Alexander L. Crosby

Georgia—C. H. Haas

Hawaii—M. L. Landgraf

North Carolina—Lawrence Hochheimer, Elizabeth Lawrence, Lionel Melvin

Tennessee—Ben. Channell (Vanderbilt University), Cleo Fitch

South Carolina—University of South Carolina, W. T. Batson

From the northeast:

Maine—Erma Denzer, Grace Babb

Vermont—Elizabeth Clarke

Massachusetts—Paul Leslie

New York—H. Lincoln Foster

New Jersey—A. L. Crosby

Connecticut—Eleanor Brinckerhoff, John S. Gallagher, Lawrence Hochheimer

Pennsylvania—University of Pennsylvania herbarium sheets, Josephine Breneman, Elizabeth Nimmo, W. A. Reese, Virginia Thomas, Edgar T. Wherry, Pennsylvania State University, Norman C. Deno

There are many more who sent plants to me whose names are not mentioned because the plant was a duplicate or occasionally because no name was attached to the packet. I have tried to send each donor a personal note of thanks, but this in no way can express my deep gratitude for their help, nor the sense I feel that this is a cooperative effort and that each of them deserves credit (but no blame!) for a share in the production of this book.

My sister, Elsa Menke, provided valued help. My husband, Eugene Henry Klaber, gave me the benefit of his constructive criticism of both text and illustrations as he had through the years. He lifted many burdens from my shoulders so that I could concentrate on the job, and was patient and understanding beyond words.

I could not, even with all the above-mentioned help, have written this book without the assistance and sustained encouragement of Dr. Norman H. Russell.

DORETTA KLABER

A NOTE FROM THE PUBLISHER

Doretta Klaber died on May 23, 1974, a few weeks after she had checked the proofs of this book. She was 86 years old. The color proofs were later checked by Dr. Norman H. Russell and the revised proofs were read by Alexander L. Crosby.

INTRODUCTION

One day I decided that I wanted to know our native violets so that I could call them by name and not just nod and smile as I went by. I soon discovered that the Violaceae are a complex family.

I looked for help from books. I found Ezra Brainerd's monographs on the violet, written in the 1920s, and I found his daughter's book, Mrs. Viola Brainerd Baird's, illustrated in color by F. Schuyler Mathews. But her book had been published in only 1000 copies, and one could not get it for study, and while the paintings were most attractive, there was little detail shown. Some of Brainerd's work has become dated over the years, and now another botanist, Dr. Norman H. Russell, has been studying violets intensively for years and is considered our present authority.

To supplement my incomplete knowledge, I asked Dr. Russell whether he would be willing to help me with the identification of the plants. His response and cooperation have been more than generous. He has examined every drawing, read the manuscript for botanical accuracy and clarity, and has helped with comments and encouragement —sometimes finding it difficult to fit my demands into his busy schedule. He sent me his monograph printed in March 1965, *Violets of the Central and Eastern United States: an Introductory Survey,* and it has been my constant reference book.

There are any number of botanical treatises on the violet, written by botanists or by those who first discovered a native violet, but these are technical papers not written for the general public.

So, at first only for myself, but later to pass on what I learned to others, the only answer seemed to be for me to collect plants of the wild species from all over the country and to draw them from life, in color, showing both flower and seed stages, root system and manner of growth. This, of course, does not include the hybrids (the crosses between any two species) which are legion. I include a few of these that were formerly thought to be species, so that the seeker for them may find them. In a book of this sort it doesn't seem feasible to add the many species synonyms that have been discarded over the years. Where they are still prevalent in some parts of the country, I include them parenthetically or in the index.

With all the violets there are so many ifs and buts. You will look in vain in this book for many violets you may come across in your wanderings. There will be different cutting or toothing of the leaves; there will be, as you can see from the drawings, many colors or shades of colors of the flowers, and sometimes of the leaves of a given species.

With one or two exceptions, the plants shown are those identified as species by Brainerd, other botanists, and now Dr. Russell. These include all species now accepted.

To obtain live specimens of all the violets that I could not find locally, I requested the help of the

Departments of Agriculture of all of the 50 states, of many of the Botanical Departments of the State Universities, of a number of commercial nurseries that deal in wild flowers, and of many friends and acquaintances around the country. Most of the plants have been sent airmail, in closed polyethylene bags, soilless, and shipped in cardboard boxes. They fade fast when exposed to the house air, and in some instances I have had to plant them out in the garden and wait for another spring to see them and draw them in bloom.

After my preliminary studies I realized why violets are difficult to identify. One reason is that most species will hybridize with any other violets growing nearby, and the hybrids will show characteristics of both parents. Also, the spring and summer appearances of many of the violets are quite different; the early leaves that appear with the flowers are usually small, then increase in size as the flowers fade and go to seed. But perhaps the greatest difficulty is the variation frequently found in the same species. A single plant will have leaves of different shapes, while plants of one species will vary depending on location, soil, moisture, and amount of sun and shade. For example, I dug *Viola conspersa* from a sunny bank on a roadside, where it was a compact plant not more than three inches high, covered with handsome blue flowers. I planted it in rich, shady woods and the plant grew to 12 inches, spread widely, but still bore a profusion of its distinctive blue flowers. The flowers, too, will vary in color and size, depending on the soil, the time of year, or perhaps just a natural variation. Many violets have a second blooming in fall, but these are usually considerably smaller flowers than their spring form.

There are nevertheless many easily identifiable species, and there are special features that distinguish others that at first may seem confusing.

Cleistogamous flowers (those that never open but fertilize themselves in the bud) are typical of violets. Not all violets produce them, but they may be found on most species as shorter, lower buds, perhaps half-buried in the soil. They become erect as the seedpods develop, and when ripe, the pods open and throw the seeds far and wide.

Violets have other ways of increasing themselves, perhaps the rarest being for the open flowers themselves to go to seed. Instead of cleistogenes they may increase by runners that root along their stems or at their ends and form new plants; or the clumps may increase so that they are easily pulled apart into divisions; or they may form stolons (underground stems) that then send up new growth near the parent plant. In the diagrams of the glossary I have tried to simplify all these words.

Some of our violets are thought to have emigrated here in ages past by the land bridge from Asia. Two of the species described, *Viola odorata* and *Viola tricolor,* are introduced plants that have become naturalized in some parts of the country.

There is probably no state in the Union where wild violets cannot be found. They grow in fields and woods, in deserts and mountains, in bogs and along water courses, in arctic and tropical country. Emphasizing their widespread nature is the fact that both Hawaii and Alaska are represented in this book.

Ultimately, I found that there are three characteristics that are of most help in identifying a given species:

First is color. Besides the common purple violet, there are all shades of lavender and blue; there are white, bicolor, yellow, and even pink and red forms.

Second is the great variation in leaf form: some with the typical heart-shaped leaf of the most common violets; others with cut foliage, like the bird's-foot violet; and still others with lobed leaves, lance-shaped leaves, primrose-like leaves, and so on. There is, in fact, so much variation, that to avoid confusion I have arbitrarily divided them into cut-leaved and uncut forms.

Third, the manner of growth of violets shows two distinct forms. On many, the flowers and leaves come up from the ground on single stalks—the kind we usually think of when we speak of violets. These are called *stemless violets.* Others grow on stems from which leaves and flowers branch. These are called *stemmed violets.*

Thus I have three ways of dividing violets so that one can begin to identify them. This scheme does not represent all the differences, but it makes a good start. That is how I am presenting them in this book: by their color, whether the leaf is cut or uncut, and whether they are of the stemmed or stemless group.

For the convenience of the reader, I repeat the listing of groups shown in the Contents, which is the key for identification.

KEY

Group I	Stemless Blue Uncut
Group II	Stemless Blue Cut-leaved
Group III	Stemmed Blue Uncut
Group IV	Stemmed Blue Cut-leaved
Group V	Stemless White Uncut
Group VI	Stemmed White Uncut
Group VII	Stemless Yellow Uncut
Group VIII	Stemmed Yellow Uncut
Group IX	Stemmed Yellow Cut-leaved

The dominant color has been used to identify the plants. For instance, in *Viola pedata* one form is lavender, another form bi-color—purple and lavender. This is listed as "blue," a catch-all for all the lavenders, purples, violets, and other tones. Many of the violets have *forms* of differing colors, but if the *type* is "blue" it is so listed. The same is true of the white and yellow-flowered violets. Very few violets are really blue, but it is the term that has been commonly associated with them so I have used it rather than "purple."

GLOSSARY

With definitions according to Gray or Webster and translations of violet names

Acaulescent	Stemless, or apparently so, or with stem subterranean
Acute	Terminating with a sharp or well-defined angle
Adunca	Hooked-spur
Affinis	Affiliated
Anther	The polleniferous part of a stamen
Appressed	Lying close and flat against, as auricle against a capsule
Arvensis	Of the field
Ascending	Rising somewhat obliquely or curving upward
Auricle	An ear-shaped appendage
Axil	The angle formed by a leaf or branch with the stem
Bearded	Bearing hairs; on violets, usually on lateral petals at center of flower
Bract	A more or less modified leaf subtending a flower or belonging to an inflorescence or sometimes cauline
Bractlet	A bract on the pedicel of a flower
Calyx	The outer perianth of the flower
Capsule	Seedpod
Caulescent	Having a manifest stem above ground
Cauline	Belonging to the stem
Cleistogamous	Fertilized in the bud without the opening of the flower
Cleistogene	A cleistogamous flower
Connate	United; used especially of like structures joined from the start
Conspersa	Speckled (An accepted but inapt name for *V. conspersa*)
Cordate	Heart-shaped with the point upward
Cormlike	Like a solid bulb
Corolla	The inner perianth of distinct or connate petals
Creeping	Running along at or near the surface of the ground and rooting
Crenate	Dentate with the teeth much rounded
Cucullata	Hooded or cowl-shaped
Cuneate	Wedge-shaped; triangular with the acute angle downward
Deciduous	Not persistent; not evergreen
Decumbent	Reclining but with summit ascending
Deltoid	Shaped like the Greek letter delta; triangular
Dentate	Toothed, usually with the teeth directed outward
Depressed	Somewhat flattened from above
Dilatata	Larger and more widely spaced
Dissected	Cut or divided into numerous sections

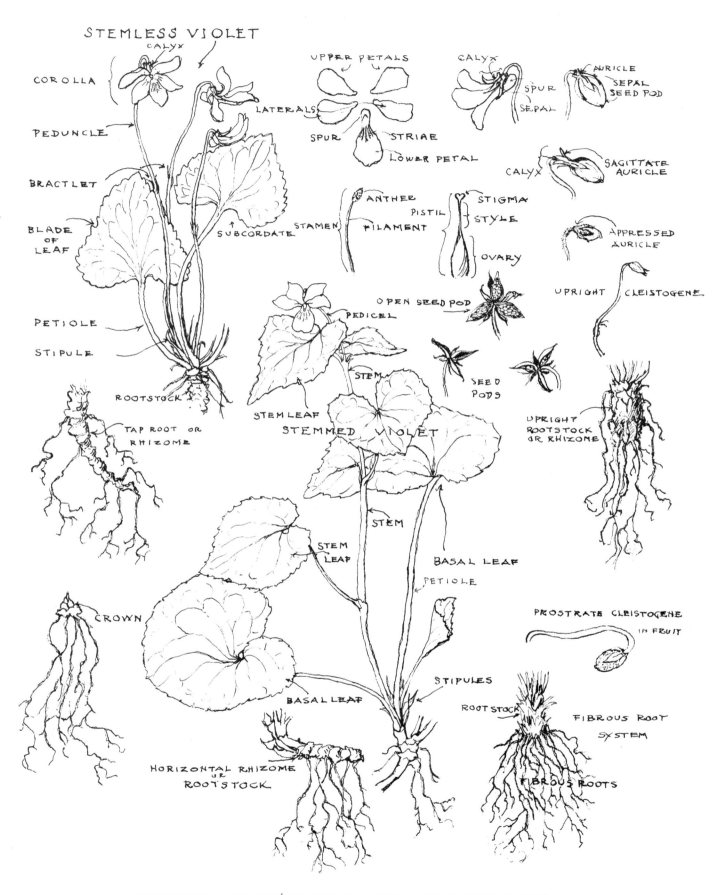

STEMLESS VIOLET

CALYX

COROLLA

PEDUNCLE

BRACTLET

BLADE
OF
LEAF

SUBCORDATE

PETIOLE

STIPULE

ROOTSTOCK

TAP ROOT OR
RHIZOME

UPPER PETALS

LATERALS

SPUR   STRIAE

LOWER PETAL

ANTHER
PISTIL
STAMEN   FILAMENT

CALYX

SPUR

SEPAL

CALYX

STIGMA

STYLE

OVARY

OPEN SEED POD

PEDICEL

STEM

STEM LEAF

STEMMED VIOLET

SEED
PODS

AURICLE
SEPAL
SEED POD

SAGITTATE
AURICLE

APPRESSED
AURICLE

UPRIGHT CLEISTOGENE

UPRIGHT
ROOTSTOCK
OR RHIZOME

CROWN

STEM
LEAF

STEM

BASAL LEAF

PETIOLE

PROSTRATE CLEISTOGENE
IN FRUIT

BASAL LEAF

STIPULES

ROOT STOCK

FIBROUS ROOT
SYSTEM

HORIZONTAL RHIZOME
OR
ROOTSTOCK

FIBROUS ROOTS

STEMMED AND STEMLESS PLANTS AND THEIR PARTS

Emarginata	Having a shallow notch at the extremity	*Lineariloba*	Long narrow lobes
Entire	Without toothing or division	*Lines*	Striae
Epipsela	Growing on mosses	*Lobate*	Having lobes
Eriocarpa	With woolly capsule	*Lobe*	Any section of an organ, especially if rounded
Esculenta	Edible		
		Midrib	The central or main rib of a leaf
Fimbriate	Fringed		
Floriferous	Flower-bearing	*Nephrophylla*	Kidney-shaped leaves
		Nerve	A simple or unbranched vein or slender rib
Genera	Plural of genus		
Genus	A group of species	*Node*	The place upon the stem which normally bears a leaf or whorl of leaves
Glabella	Hairless or smooth		
Glabrous	Smooth; not rough, pubescent, or hairy		

Halberd-shaped	Same as hastate	*Obcordate*	Inverted heart-shape
Hastate	Like an arrow-head, but with the basal lobes pointing outward nearly at right angles	*Oblanceolate*	Lanceolate with the broadest part towards the apex
Heart-shaped	Ovate with two rounded lobes and a sinus at the base; commonly used to define such a base	*Oblong*	Longer than broad with nearly parallel sides
		Obovate	Inverted ovate
Hirsute	Pubescent with short or stiff hairs	*Obovoid*	Having the form of an inverted egg
Hybrid	A cross breed of two species	*Obtuse*	Blunt or rounded at the end
		Occidentalis	Of the west
Incised	Cut sharply and irregularly, more or less deeply	*Ocellata*	Marked like an eye
		Orbicular	Circular
Incognita	Unrecognized	*Ovate*	Egg-shaped
Inflorescence	The flowering part of a plant, and especially the mode of its arrangement	*Ovoid*	A solid with an oval outline
Integrifolia	Entire leaved	*Pallens*	Pale
Introduced	Brought intentionally from another region	*Palmate* (leaf)	Radiately lobed or divided
		Palustrine	Of or growing in marshes
Irregular (flower)	Showing inequality in the size, form, or union of its different parts	*Papilionaceous* (corolla)	Having a standard, wings and keel, as in a pea-shaped flower
		Pectinate	Pinnatifid with narrow, closely set segments; comb-like
Lanceolate	Shaped like a lance-head, several times longer than wide, broadest above the base, narrowed to the apex	*Pedate*	Palmately divided or parted, with the lateral segments two-cleft
		Pedatifida	Divided pedately
Linear	Long and narrow with parallel margins	*Pedicel*	The support of a single flower in a group

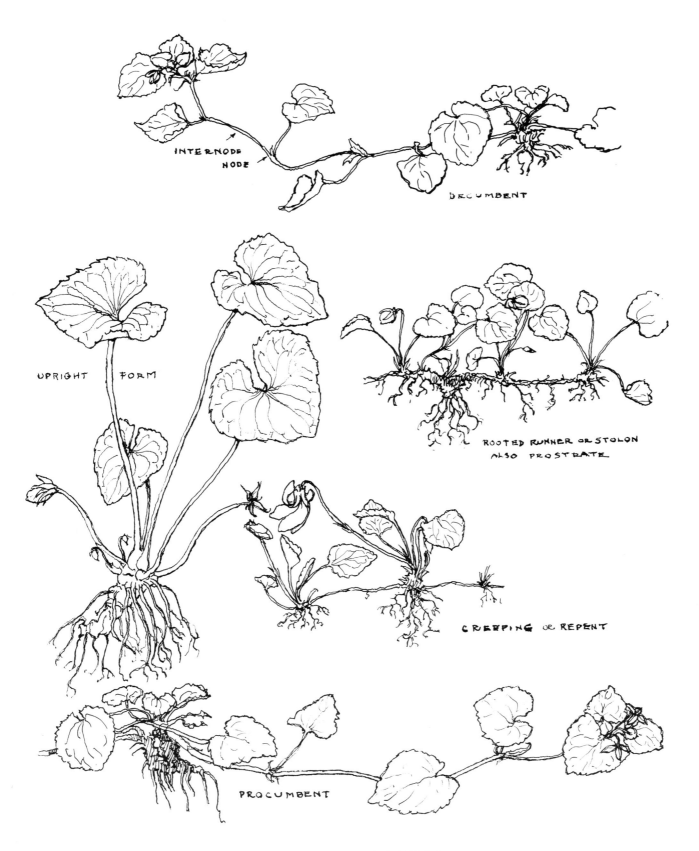

INTERNODE
NODE

DECUMBENT

UPRIGHT FORM

ROOTED RUNNER OR STOLON
ALSO PROSTRATE

CREEPING OR REPENT

PROCUMBENT

FORMS OF GROWTH

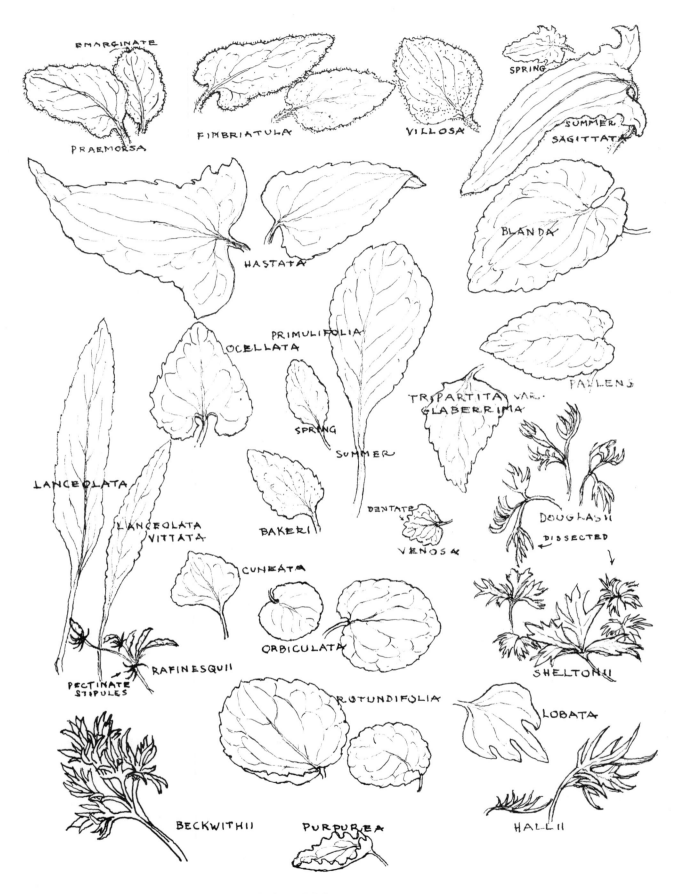

LEAF SHAPES AND TOOTHING

Peduncle	A primary flower-stalk, supporting either a cluster or a solitary flower	*Sarmentose*	Producing prostrate runners
		Scabrous	Rough to the touch
Perennial	Lasting year after year	*Scape*	A peduncle rising from the ground, naked or without proper foliage
Persistent	Long-lasting, as a calyx upon the fruit, leaves through winter, etc.	*Segment*	One of the parts of a leaf or other like organ that is cleft or divided
Petal	A division of the corolla		
Petiole	The footstalk of a leaf		
Pistil	The seed-bearing organ of the flower	*Sepal*	A division of the calyx
		Septemloba	Seven-lobed
Pod	The seed-pod or fruit	*Septentrionalis*	Northern
Praemorse	Appearing as if bitten off	*Serrate*	Having sharp teeth pointing forward
Pratincola	Growing in meadows		
Primulifolia	Primrose-leaved	*Silky*	Covered with close-pressed, soft and straight pubescence
Procumbent	Lying on the ground but without rooting at the nodes		
		Simple	Of one piece, not compound
Proliferous	Producing offshoots	*Sinus*	The cleft or recess between two lobes
Prostrate	Lying flat upon the ground		
Pubescent	Covered with hairs, especially if short, soft, and down-like	*Smooth*	Without roughness or pubescence
		Species	A distinct kind
Reflexed	Abruptly bent or turned downward	*Spur*	A hollow, sac-like, or tubular extension of the lower petal of a violet; usually contains nectar
Reniform	Kidney-shaped		
Repent	Creeping; prostrate and rooting at the nodes	*Stalk*	The stem of any organ as pedicel, peduncle, petiole
Reticulate	In the form of net-work; net-veined	*Stamen*	One of the pollen-bearing organs of the flower
Retuse	With a shallow notch at a rounded apex	*Stem*	The main ascending axis of the plant
Revolute	Rolled backward from the margins or apex	*Stigma*	That part of the pistil through which fertilization by the pollen is effected
Rhizome	Any prostrate or subterranean stem, usually rooting at the nodes and becoming erect at the apex	*Stipule*	An appendage at the base of the petiole or on each side of its insertion; the three parts of a complete leaf are blade, petiole, stipules (usually two)
Root	The underground part of a plant which supplies it with nourishment		
Rootstock	Same as a rhizome	*Stolon*	A runner, or any basal branch that is disposed to root
Rostrata	(Having a beak) Long-spurred		
Rotundifolia	Round-leaved	*Striate*	Marked with fine longitudinal lines or ridges, as on lower petals
Rugulosa	Wrinkled		
Runner	A filiform or very slender stolon	*Sub-cordate*	Slightly heart-shaped
Sagittate	Shaped like an arrow-head, the basal lobe directed downward	*Trachellifolia*	Refers to woody tissues or tubes
		Triloba	Three-lobed

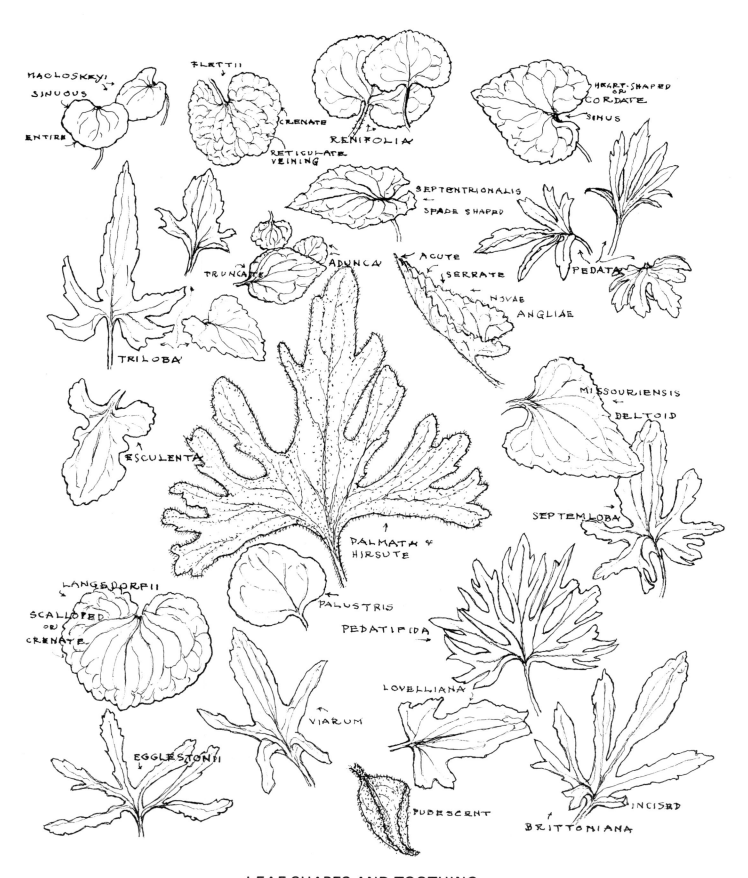

LEAF SHAPES AND TOOTHING

Trinervata	Three-nerved	*Venosa*	Conspicuously veined (on leaves)
Truncate	Ending abruptly, as if cut off transversely	*Viarum*	Probably, growing along the way
		Villous	Bearing long and soft hairs
Vallicola	Growing in valleys		
Veined	On flowers, same as striate	*Woolly*	Clothed with long, matted hairs

GROUP I

STEMLESS BLUE
UNCUT

Violas sororia
     cucullata
     affinis
     missouriensis
     floridana
     Langloisii
     septentrionalis
     novae-angliae
     pratincola
     nephrophylla
     Langsdorfii
     fimbriatula
     villosa
     hirsutula
     sagittata
     esculenta
     Lovelliana

VIOLA SORORIA Willd.

(PAPILIONACEA Pursh.)

The Common, Dooryard or Sister-Violet

Plates I and II

We open this book with *Viola sororia,* the 'Sister-Violet,' because it is the commonest species in the United States. It is found in areas from the east coast to the central and upper midwest. "That's what I call a violet" is the reaction of many people to the purple one shown on Plate II.

In the midwest and usually in wooded sections in the east, most of the forms of *Viola sororia* show a varying amount of hairiness on either leaf-stalks, back of leaves, edges of leaves, or all three. Here in Pennsylvania in the open part of my garden they are all hairless. As you can see on page 28 and Plates I and II, there is also great variation in the size of the leaves, which especially in the shade grow tall and large as the season advances. A rather open sinus (usually) characterizes the leaves and the large upright cleistogenes are very noticeable in summer.

As Dr. Russell pointed out, plants formerly assigned to *V. papilionacea* prove to be smooth forms of *V. sororia*. This view has been generally accepted by other botanists, so that our common dooryard violet, so long known as *V. papilionacea,* is now called *V. sororia* or 'Sister-Violet' because it hybridizes and grades into any other species growing nearby.

The normal purple color may vary to red, striped, dotted as in 'Freckles,' purple-centered as in the 'Confederate Violet' (*V. priceana*) and other shades of blue, and white. It spreads rapidly by prolific seeding and can make an excellent groundcover where appropriate.

The pure white form, *Viola s. albiflora,* and the albino form on Plate II do not seem to spread with the abandon of the others. For instance, I brought a single plant of the 'Confederate Violet' when I moved to Pennsylvania from Washington, D. C. In no time it was all over the garden. There have been many beauties among the seedlings, such as the one pictured, the normal color being somewhat paler.

None of the violets in this group needs any special attention. They will grow wherever you want them—in sun or shade or semi-shade—and many times they will grow where you don't want them.

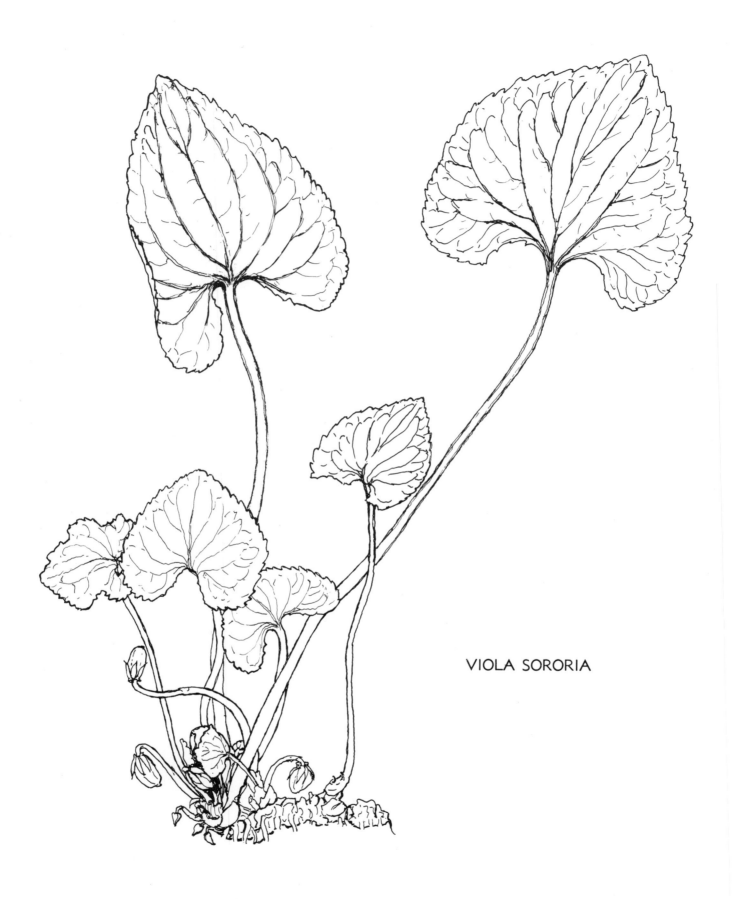

VIOLA SORORIA

VIOLA CUCULLATA Ait.

Blue Marsh Violet

Plate III

If you were walking in a marshy place in spring, your footsteps would probably be arrested if you came across the lovely lavender flowers with their deep violet centers—the typical form of *Viola cucullata.* Is this just another form of the dooryard violet *V. sororia?* But no, on closer examination you notice that the flowers are carried well above the leaves, not equalling them in height as most sororias do. They have narrower and fewer flowers, each standing gracefully by itself.

This is a widespread species with a long season of bloom, found from New England to Georgia and Arkansas. There is a rare white form and a bicolor is known—white with a small violet center, and a large pale-blue hybrid is frequently found.

In summer and fall *V. cucullata* is easily identified by the long slender shape of the cleistogamous flowers and the extended ears of the sepals. The capsules are green with dark seeds when ripe.

The leaves vary in shape as most violets do, being heart-shaped to kidney-shaped with wavy toothing. They have a tendency to curl in upon themselves as they age and the sinus is usually narrower than that of a sororia. They are smooth but sometimes might be lightly pubescent. Like most plants, they grow taller in shade than in sun, but while the leaves become large they rarely reach the big size of some sororias. The rootstock is thick and scaly; its appearance is governed by the amount of moisture in the soil.

This is a wonderful violet for a moist, shady location, but spreads too rapidly to be trusted among choice plants. It is a close relative of another bog plant, *V. nephrophylla,* and their habitats overlap in New England.

Violets are edible, and *V. cucullata* seems to be a special favorite of little beasts and bugs. Sometimes it is difficult to find a whole leaf.

VIOLA CUCULLATA

VIOLA AFFINIS Le Conte

Affiliated Violet

Plate IV

This is one of our most common violets but it is not easy to identify. If you left the bog where you found *V. cucullata* and wandered into the woods, you might well come across *V. affinis,* and as you glanced at it might say, "Oh, another *sororia"* or, "It seems *V. cucullata* grows here too." But if you stop and observe it you will see that the leaves are rather small and triangular in appearance, more so than the other two, and the sinus is usually v-shaped. The leaves look smooth but may have some hairs on their edges or on the basal lobes. Later the leaves enlarge but never get so big as *V. sororia* or *V. cucullata.*

The flowers are lavender with a lighter eye—not violet-colored like the typical *V. sororia,* nor dark-eyed like *V. cucullata.* The cleistogenes have small appressed auricles to the sepals, not markedly long ones like *V. cucullata.* The rootstock is heavy with many convolutions. *V. rosacea* (Brainerd) is a rosy-red form of *V. affinis.*

Russell considers *V. affinis* one of a complex of five violets: *V. affinis* in the northeast, *V. missouriensis* in the midwest, *V. floridana* in the southeast, *V. Langloisii* in the southern midwest, and *V. viarum* (Group II) in the far midwest. Where these plants meet geographically they usually grade into each other.

There is no difficulty in growing *V. affinis* in any good woodland soil.

31

VIOLA AFFINIS

Plate I

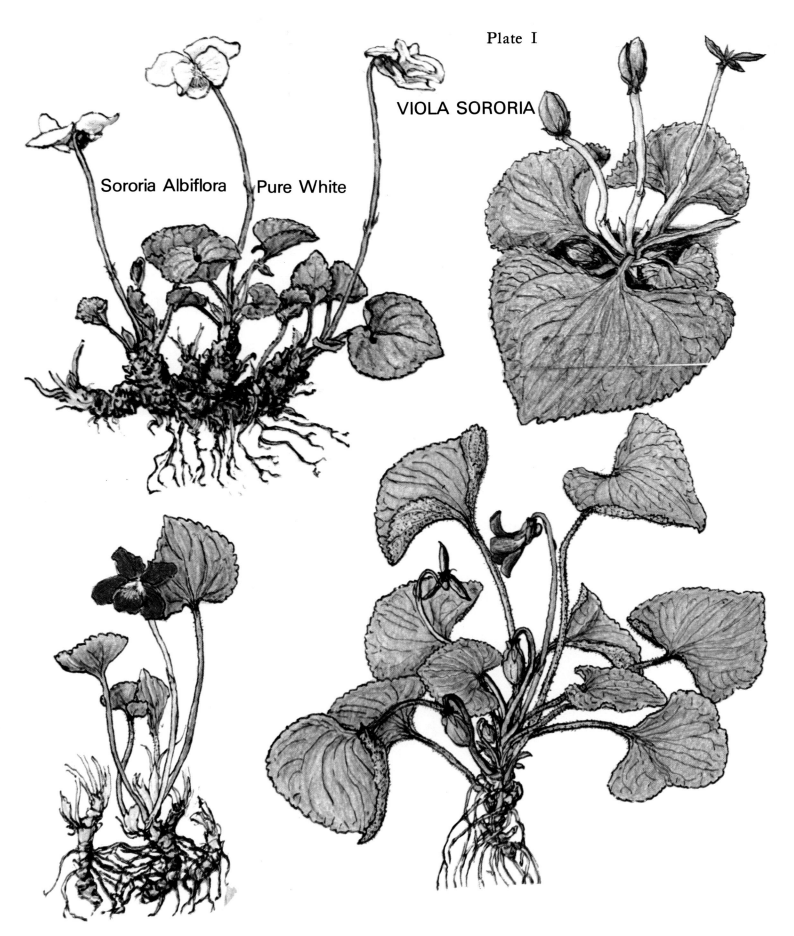

VIOLA SORORIA

Sororia Albiflora   Pure White

Plate II

VIOLA SORORIA

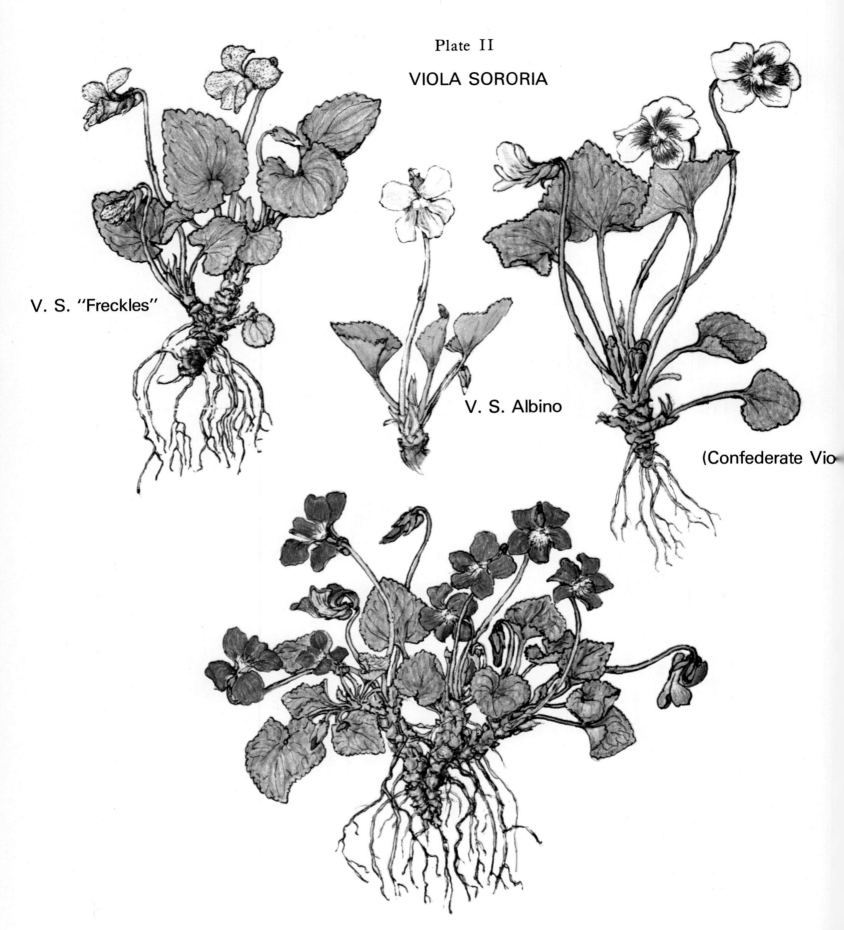

V. S. "Freckles"

V. S. Albino

(Confederate Vio

34

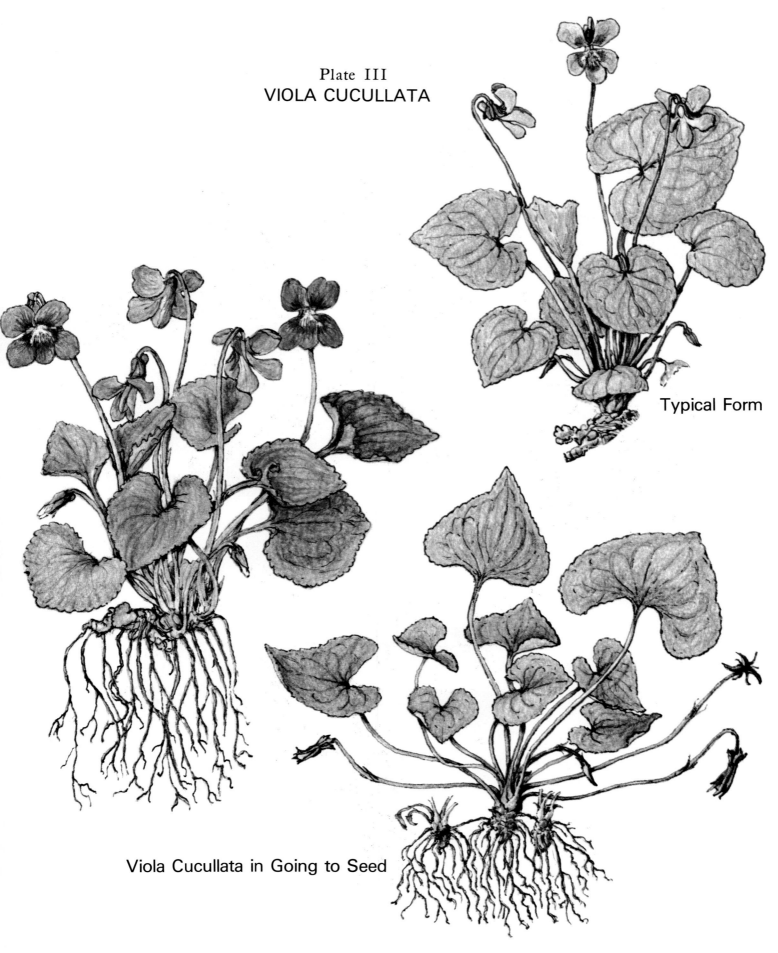

Plate III
VIOLA CUCULLATA

Typical Form

Viola Cucullata in Going to Seed

35

Plate IV

VIOLA AFFINIS

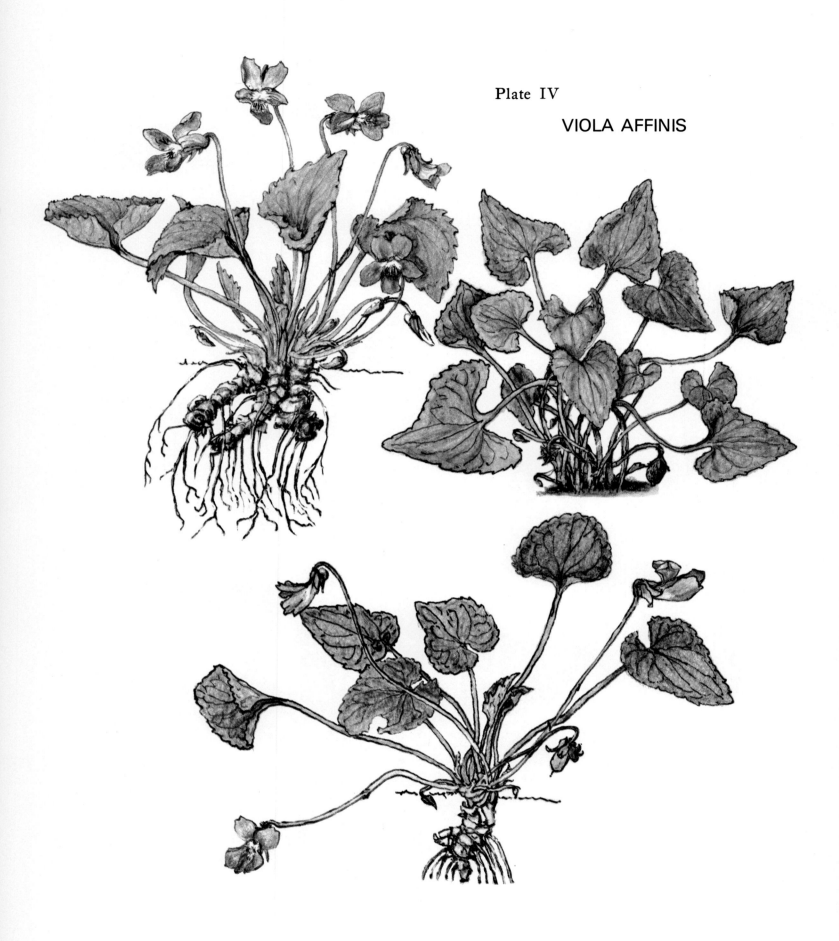

Plate V

VIOLA MISSOURIENSIS

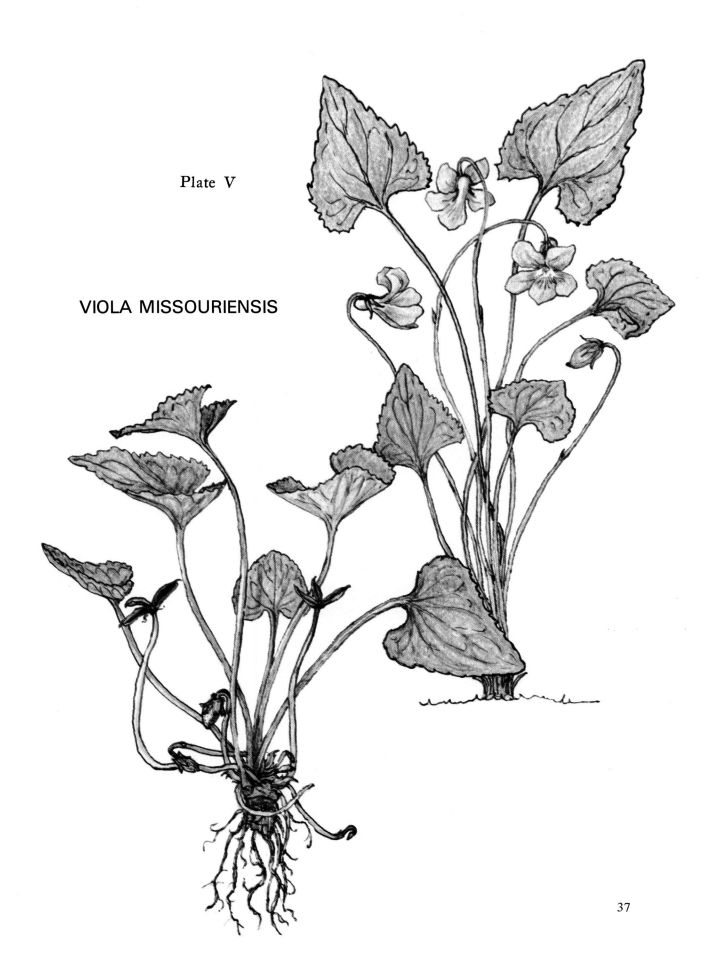

Plate VI

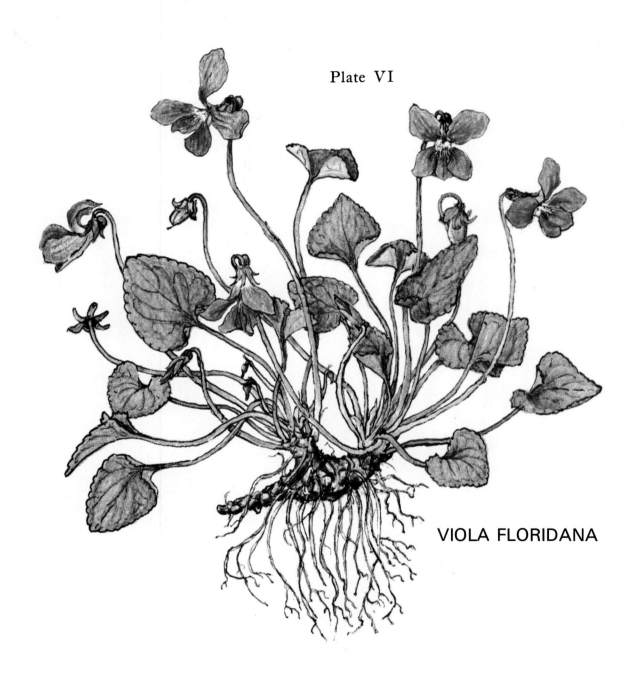

VIOLA FLORIDANA

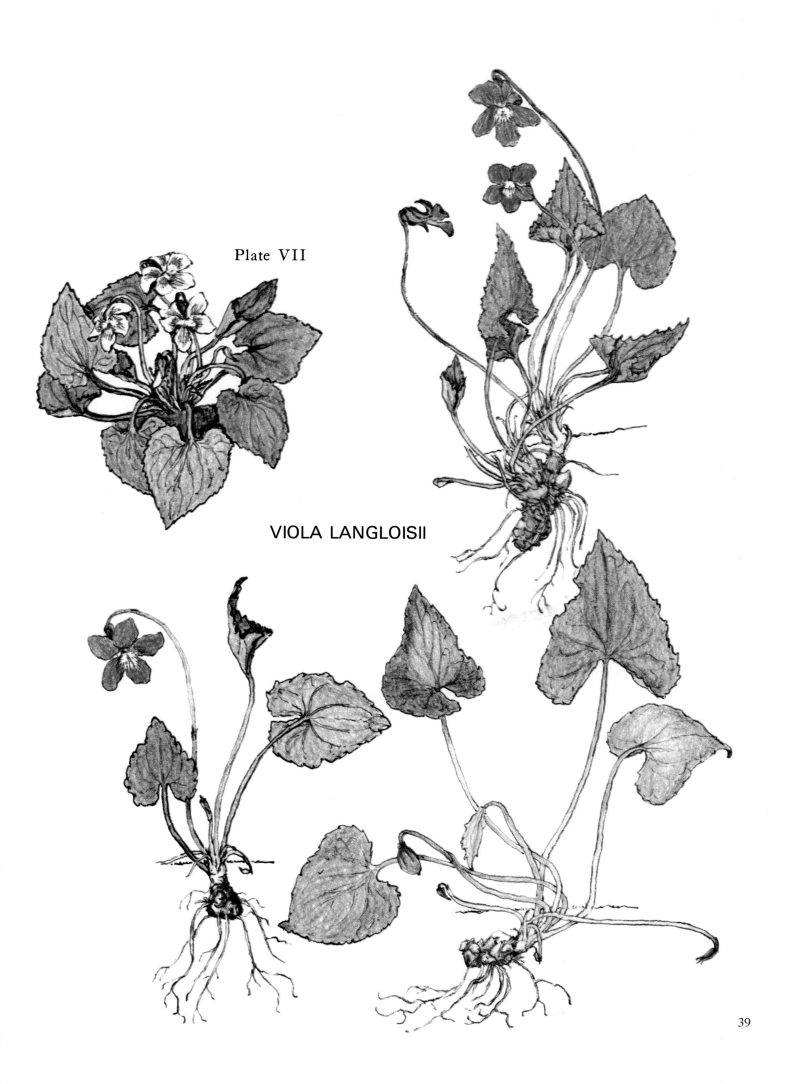

Plate VII

VIOLA LANGLOISII

Plate VIII

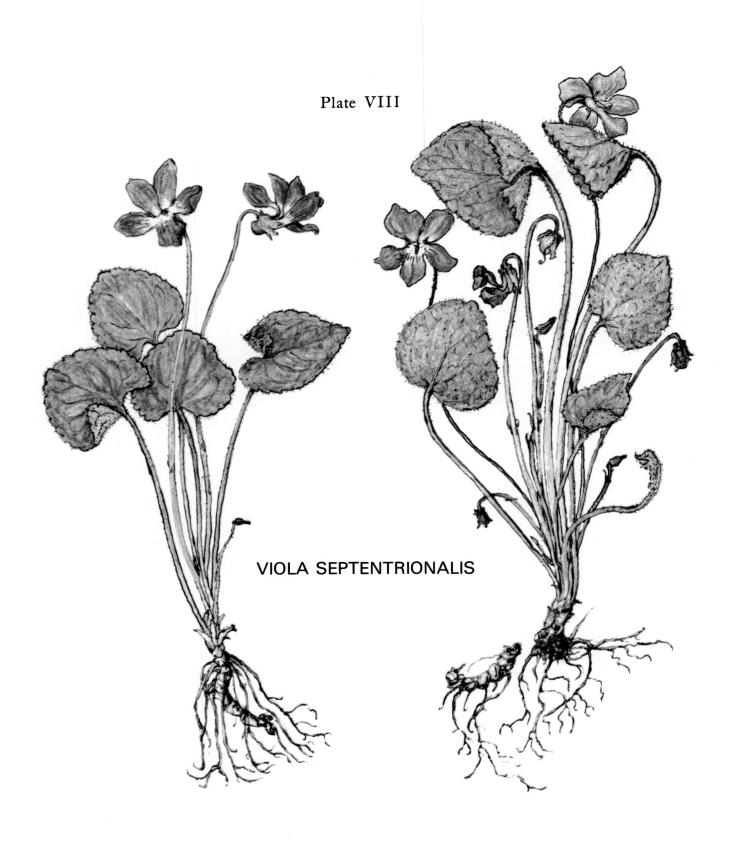

VIOLA SEPTENTRIONALIS

Plate IX

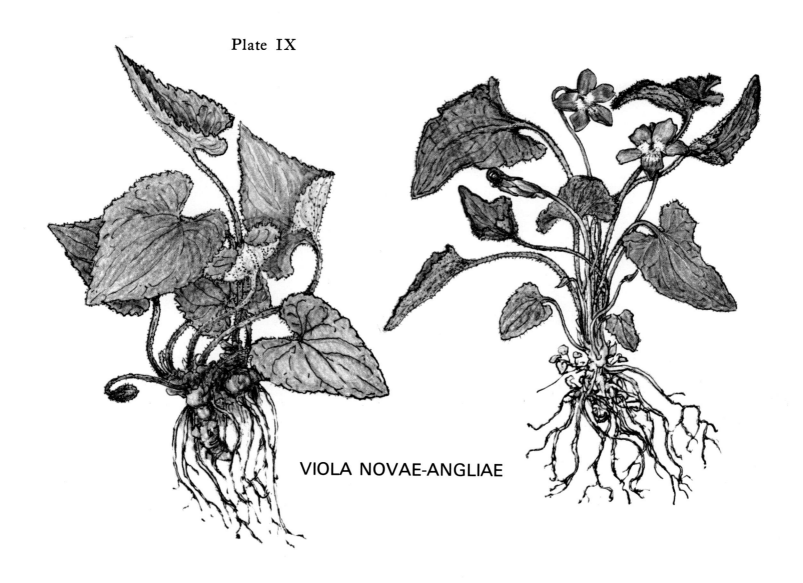

VIOLA NOVAE-ANGLIAE

Plate X

VIOLA PRATINCOLA

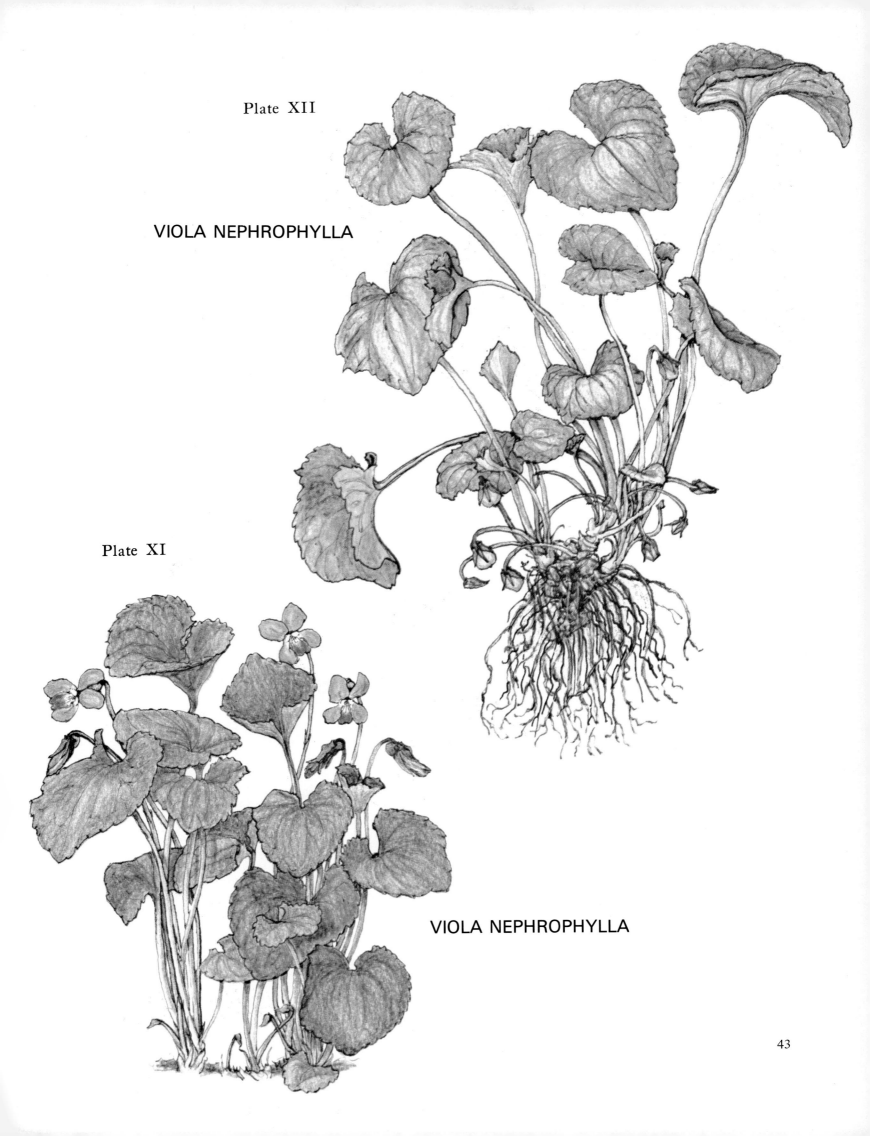

Plate XII

VIOLA NEPHROPHYLLA

Plate XI

VIOLA NEPHROPHYLLA

43

Plate XIII

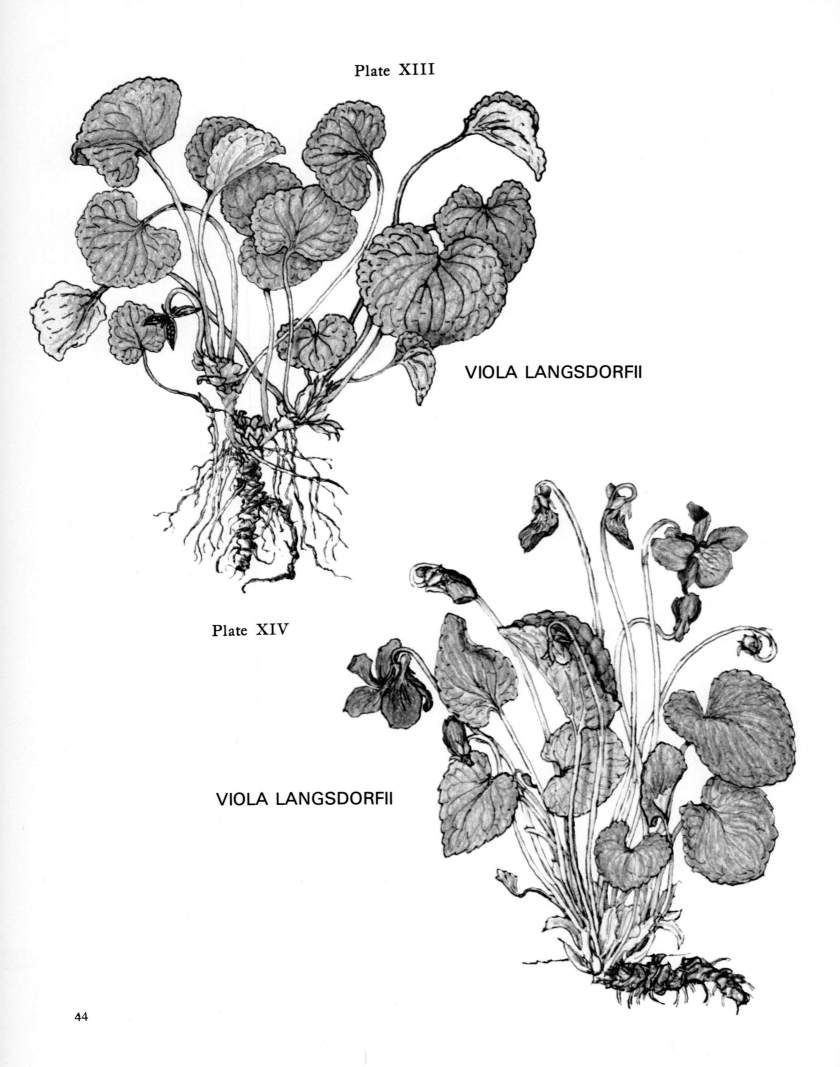

VIOLA LANGSDORFII

Plate XIV

VIOLA LANGSDORFII

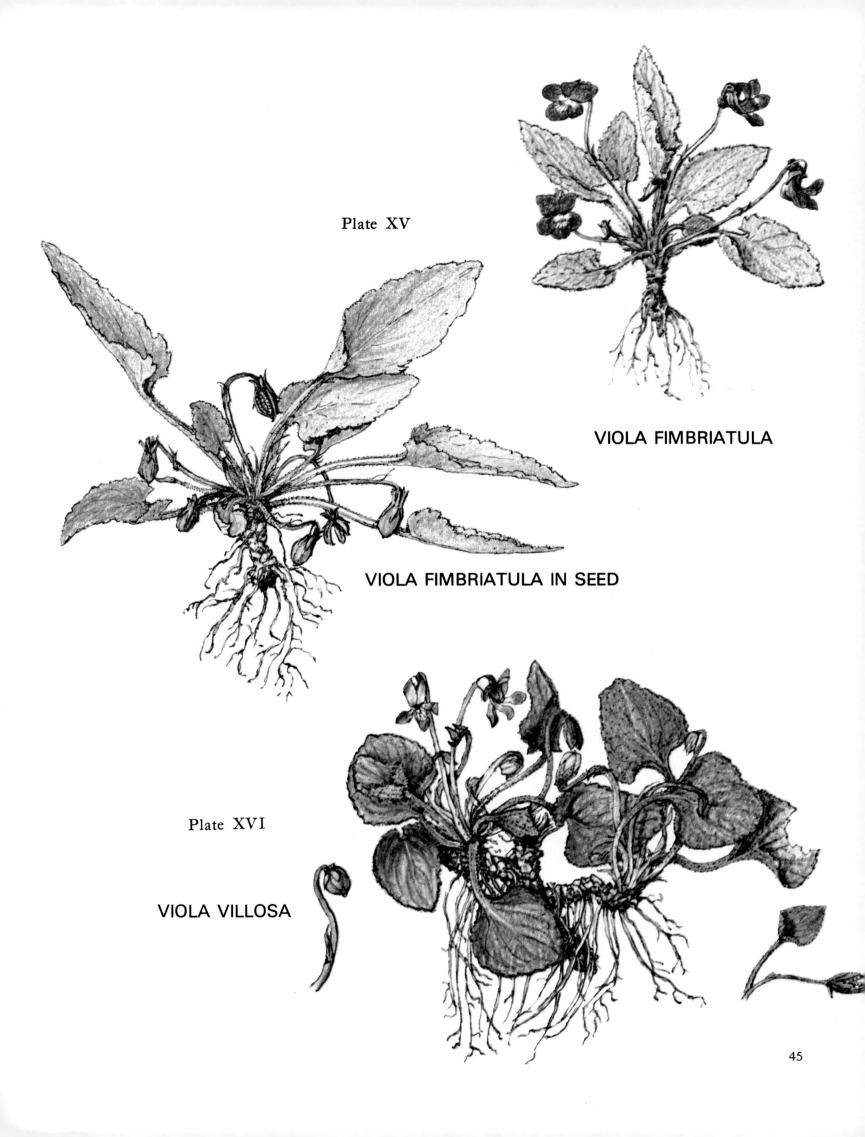

Plate XV

VIOLA FIMBRIATULA

VIOLA FIMBRIATULA IN SEED

Plate XVI

VIOLA VILLOSA

45

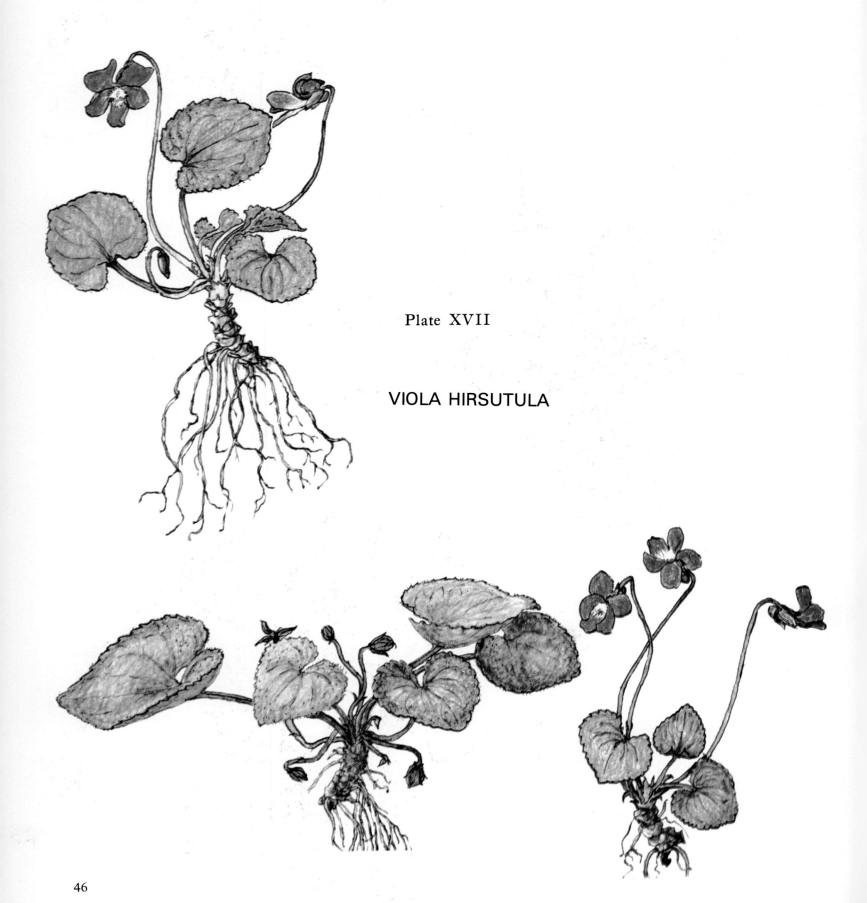

Plate XVII

VIOLA HIRSUTULA

Plate XVIII

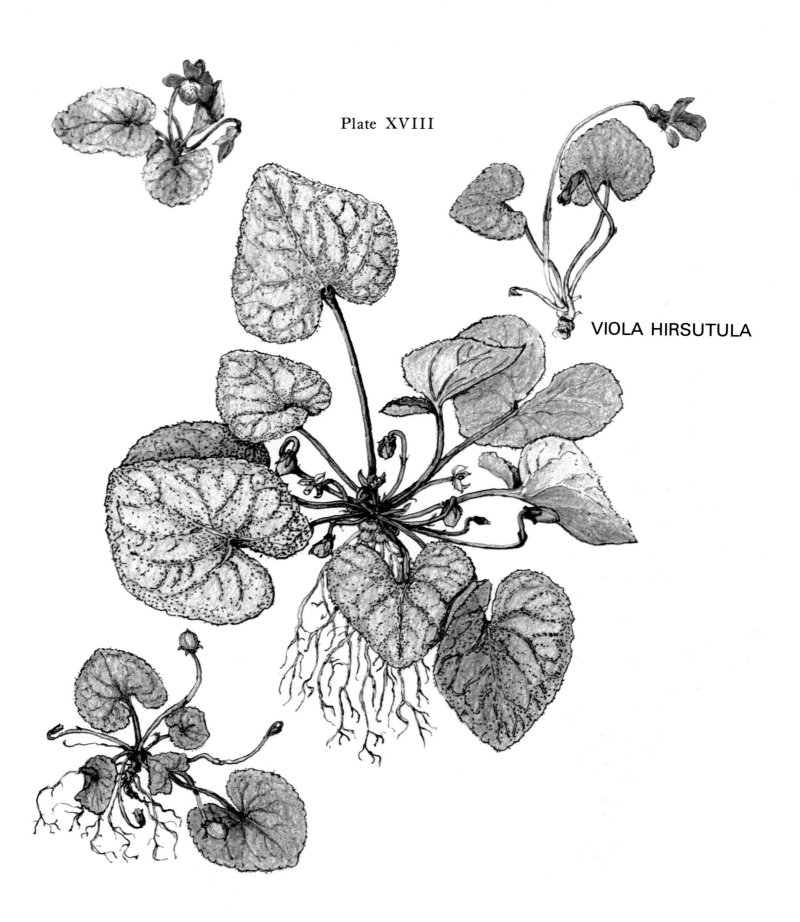

VIOLA HIRSUTULA

Plate XIX

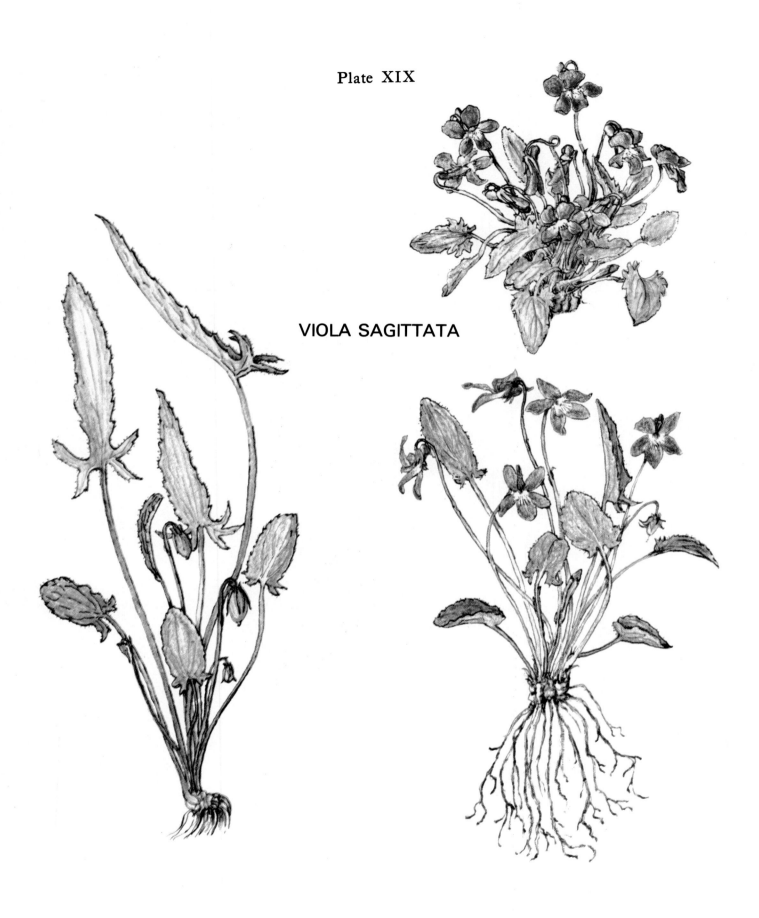

VIOLA SAGITTATA

VIOLA MISSOURIENSIS Greene

The Missouri Violet

Plate V

The summer plant I had of *Viola missouriensis* did not bloom—or I missed it in the spring rush. So I asked the curator of the Missouri Botanical Garden at St. Louis to lend me an herbarium sheet of it. He kindly and trustingly did so and I was able to make the drawing in flower with the aid of botanical descriptions.

It is the midwest member of the *affinis* complex, recognizable by its triangular leaves with triangular apexes, which usually are heart-shaped at the base and smooth. The root is short and heavy. The flowers are lavender, sometimes having a dark band around the white center, bearded, and held even with or above the leaves.

They come from moist woodland and river banks where they may colonize extensively, but they also appear as weeds in towns and villages, so we can assume that they need watching rather than coddling.

VIOLA FLORIDANA Brainerd

The Florida Violet

Plate VI

This delightful plant, found in a swamp area along a canal in North Carolina, was collected for me by a friend. It may also be found in rich, moist positions in much of the southeastern part of the country. It is another of the *affinis* complex.

Its spreading, slightly fleshy leaves are evenly scalloped and fan out below the open-patterned flowers, which are pale to deep lavender with white beards and purple lines. As with so many violets, the cleistogenes are usually prostrate at first and may be blotched with purple. The boat-shaped root seems to be characteristic.

Given sufficient well-drained moisture, *V. floridana* should be hardy in more northern climates.

VIOLA LANGLOISII Greene

Langlois' Violet

Plate VII

As you can see on Plate VII, if you compare *V. Langloisii* with *V. affinis* there are many similarities. As Russell says, *Viola Langloisii* may be just a farther southwestern variety of *V. affinis* (and related to *V. missouriensis*) but he still likes to think of it as a species. He considers *V. Langloisii* to be native only in the states bordering on the Gulf of Mexico, while *V. affinis* comes from the northeastern section of the country.

The differences that can be readily seen are the deeper purple flowers of *V. Langloisii* (though this is no guarantee as violets vary so readily), the deeper color of the leaves, especially the backs of *V. Langloisii,* which show some bronzing, and the usually longer peduncles of the flowers. Also *V. Langloisii* is found in moister positions than is *V. affinis*. The beautiful and unusual white form on Plate VII was sent me from Texas.

VIOLA LANGLOISII

VIOLA SEPTENTRIONALIS Greene

Northern Blue Violet

Plate VIII

As its name indicates *Viola septentrionalis* is found in the northern part of the United States, roughly from east to west. It may be found in moist, open woods under conifers, on mountain ledges in gravelly soil, or perhaps along the edges of thickets. Those shown came from along the edge of a pine woods in southern Maine.

The flowers, on long pubescent peduncles, usually rise above the leaves. They may be pale to deep violet with dense white beards on the three lower petals, and there is also a rare white form. The small, red-purple capsules are distinctive.

As a rule the leaves have a pointed, spade shape, and are slightly pubescent on the backs and edges as well as on the petioles.

The rootstock on older plants is short and thick and is usually branched.

As noted above, its habitats show a need for good moist soil in part shade, and its associates would indicate soil with an acid reaction.

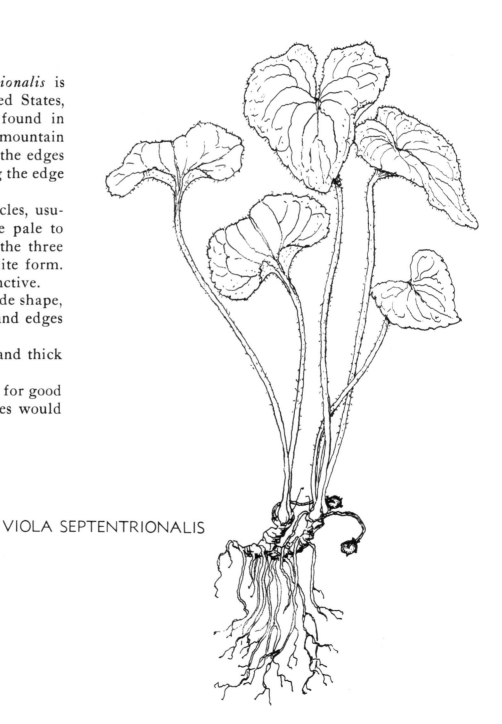

VIOLA SEPTENTRIONALIS

VIOLA NOVAE-ANGLIAE House

The New England Violet

Plate IX

Although the fall form of *V. novae-angliae* was collected in New York, the flowering plant was sent to me from Minnesota. It seems to be more widespread there, though not prolific, than in its supposed native home—in northern Maine. It is found along cold streams and sometimes in spruce fir forests.

The petioles and backs of the leaves are noticeably pubescent, and some hairs are visible along the edges of the leaves. The rather triangular leaves are reminiscent of *V. sagittata* but do not have the latter's sharp basal cutting.

The clear, clean-lavender flowers have exceptionally heavy beards on the laterals, not as noticeably so on the lower petal. The white center of the flower has a slightly greenish tinge.

A cool, moist position with good drainage is indicated.

VIOLA PRATINCOLA Greene

Blue Prairie Violet

Plate X

This midwestern violet is found in open, dry positions on the prairies, frequently on railroad embankments. My specimen came from South Dakota, and Mr. Barr, who sent it to me, says that he finds it in crevices of rocks along stream banks. It is also sometimes found as a city weed.

V. pratincola is sometimes confused with *V. sororia,* but the shape of the flower, with its usually pointed lower petal, and the tendency of the sharply pointed leaves to turn in on themselves give it a character of its own.

This rather weedy species is not fussy, though some shade is indicated.

VIOLA NEPHROPHYLLA Greene

Kidney-leaved Violet

Plates XI, XII

I found *Viola nephrophylla* one of the violets difficult to identify, probably because it is one of the most widespread, and for that reason varies greatly. It is found both east and west and in between. The plant shown came from the state of Washington and seems to differ from the eastern ones that have been described as having their flowers well above the leaves instead of equal to them or lower.

It is spoken of as a wet-ground species from the open, but has also been reported from shaded areas. Its leaves, though named "kidney-shaped," may also be pointed and heart-shaped. It is usually glabrous but sometimes has pubescence on the upper lobes. The leaves vary from a yellow-green to a deep blue-green.

But, in spite of all this, the plant is recognizable once you are familiar with it. The general feeling of the leaves is roundish, the capsules are green with dark sepals (an unusual combination), the cleistogenes, prostrate at first, gradually become erect, and the plant is very leafy with deeply veined glossy foliage. Its violet-colored flowers are deeper purple on the lower petal, white-centered and bearded. The root-system is extremely matted so that it is difficult to make out the branching heavy rootstock. The plants grow taller with age but the leaves never grow so large as do those of *V. sororia* and *V. cucullata*.

It presents no difficulties in cultivation.

VIOLA LANGSDORFII Fischer

The Alaska Violet

Plates XIII, XIV

This gorgeous violet was sent to me from Alaska. It is also found on our west coast as far south as California. For convenience, I have placed it among the stemless violets, though actually it should have a classification of its own, as it is considered intermediate between the stemless and stemmed violets. From a stout rootstock there may be several upright stemlike divisions at the top, with many large, red-striped stipules.

The flowers vary from lavender-blue to deeper violet, or can be white. They are large and rich-looking and held above the foliage. The large capsules are green. The leaves are slightly broader than long with wavy scalloping, heart-shaped base, and rounded tip.

It is found growing in moist moss on the tundra, and given a moist, well-drained position should be hardy much farther south.

VIOLA FIMBRIATULA J. E. Smith

Northern Downy Violet

Plate XV

Viola fimbriatula was brought to me from the Pocono Mountains in Pennsylvania. It was the first time I had seen it and I was enchanted. Such a soft, downy little plant, hardly recognizable as a violet when not in bloom.

The blades of the leaves are longer than their petioles, and although very soft and hairy while young, they lose some of their pubescence as they grow older.

It may be found from Nova Scotia to Wisconsin and as far south as northern Georgia, usually in rather dry, open positions.

The rootstock is vertical and scaly and becomes stout with age.

The flowers are deep violet-purple, with white centers and heavy beards; they are held above the leaves. Seed-pods are large and long-eared.

There is no difficulty in cultivating it in woodland soil in half-shade.

VIOLA VILLOSA Walt.

Southern Woolly Violet

Plate XVI

In January 1968, *Viola villosa* came to me from Texas *in bloom*. Janice Lacey said it flowers in her pine woods from November on, in any warm spell. It is another species with softly woolly foliage and delicate flowers.

The pubescence is all over the plant, rusty hairs on leaves and petioles, and more lightly on pedicels. The rootstock is almost woody, and though there are no stolons, the rootstock itself branches and spreads, sending up new tufts of plants at intervals, making a low, leafy, spreading plant. Cleistogenes were in every stage of development, a sign that it spreads rapidly in the sandy soil it prefers.

The flowers, narrow-petaled and long-faced, are a light-centered, lavender-purple—dainty in appearance except for the disproportionately large white spur. They are a notable contrast to the cozy rounded flowers of *V. fimbriatula*.

I have placed *villosa* between *fimbriatula* and *hirsutula,* which is followed by *sagittata,* so that at a glance you can see the differences. You will note the varying shapes and colors of leaves, flowers, rootstock, and seedpods, and I hope have no difficulty in telling them apart.

In a country with as varied climates as ours, it's hard to lay down the law on cultivation of any plant. But, in my long life I have raised thousands of plants from seed, and I have found that *if given an approximation of their native habitat and soil*, a great many can adapt to new surroundings and climate, as gentians from the Himalayas, for example. Of course it's easier to accustom a cold-country plant to a warmer climate than vice-versa. But violets, on the whole, are hardy.

VIOLA HIRSUTULA Brainerd

Southern Woodland Violet

Plates XVII, XVIII

In spite of its common name, the range of *Viola hirsutula* is throughout most of the eastern part of the United States, from Connecticut and New York to Alabama and Georgia. It is usually found in dry, open woods. It is the only stemless blue violet that has pubescence on the upper surface of the leaves and is glabrous below. Dr. Russell found it in Tennessee and Virginia in relatively undisturbed pine forests. It usually occurs sparingly, but may furnish most of the carpeting of the forest.

The large plant on Plate XVIII was brought to me from a Pennsylvania garden where it just "appeared." I marveled at its beautiful pattern, so reminiscent of a cyclamen leaf, with some of the same silver and purple coloring. *V. hirsutula* lives up to its name with its hairy upper surface and leaf edges. The reverse of the leaves is smooth and generally purple, especially in early spring.

The small plant, interestingly patterned, on Plate XVIII came from the University of South Carolina. It was only later that I found *V. hirsutula* growing along my own woodland path. I did not recognize it at first, for although it had the purple reverse to the leaves and some hairiness on the upper surface, it lacked the pattern.

The flowers are a rich, warm red-purple with white beards and are held above the leaves. Usually they bloom in April and May, and in my deciduous woods they are scattered, never making a groundcover. You should be able to grow them in any good woodland soil.

VIOLA SAGITTATA Ait.

The Arrow-leaved Violet

Plate XIX

Viola sagittata is an example of why I decided to show both spring and summer appearances of the violets. The contrast is striking—the kitten of spring becomes the cat of summer. It is hard to believe that it is the same plant if you have not watched it develop.

This is an eastern to midwestern species found from Maine to Georgia, Louisiana, Minnesota, and Arkansas. It grows on sunny, moist banks, and in moist meadows. Because it is such a widespread plant it makes itself at home in various other locations, with varying amounts of moisture. In the north the plants are, as a rule, said to be pubescent; in the south, glabrous. However, both the plants shown came from Pennsylvania—one pubescent, the other only slightly so. So you see!

In its early stages *V. sagittata* can be confused with *V. fimbriatula*. If you will look at Plate XV (*V. fimbriatula*) you will see that the toothing near the base of the leaves is not so pronounced, that *V. fimbriatula* is a soft, hairy plant, that the flowers are deeper toned than those of *V. sagittata* usually are, and that although *V. fimbriatula* increases in size too, it never has the tall, upright stalks of *V. sagittata*.

The flowers of *V. sagittata* bloom in April and May, and their light-violet petals are veined darker, the three lower petals white at the base and densely bearded. The cleistogenes rise on slender peduncles and have sagittate sepals.

Naturally, such an adaptable species responds readily to cultivation.

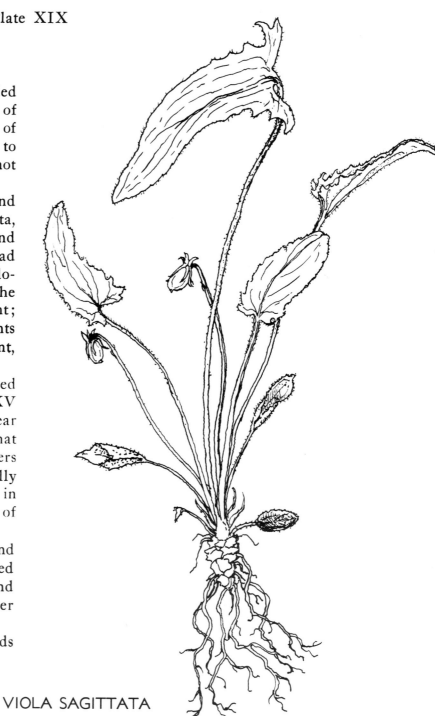

VIOLA SAGITTATA

VIOLA ESCULENTA Ell.

Edible Violet

Plate XX

Viola esculenta was sent to me in March 1967, in bloom, from Florida. It is common throughout the south from the Carolinas to Florida and to Mississippi. It is half-way between the cut-leaved and the uncut species, so I placed it with the uncut, as the early and late leaves are in this category. As the plant matures a variety of lobings occur. There are a number of distinctive points that make it easy to identify.

One distinguishing feature is the root system, the mature rootstock being crimson, thick and fleshy, and branching with age. Another, the leaves are also slightly fleshy, clean, and glabrous, with rather short and frequently prostrate petioles. The leaves as well as the flowers are edible, but this is true of most violets except the hairy ones. Certainly to wild animals, bugs, and slugs, they are "goodies" indeed.

The winged flowers, ready to fly away, are carried well above the leaves. They start with white buds but open out to a clean, pale violet with darker lines, a creamy center and white beards on the laterals. There is a white form of the flower. The seedpods are large and purplish on prostrate peduncles at first.

This violet comes from wet borders of streams and swampy areas, so well-drained moisture in sun or light shade is indicated.

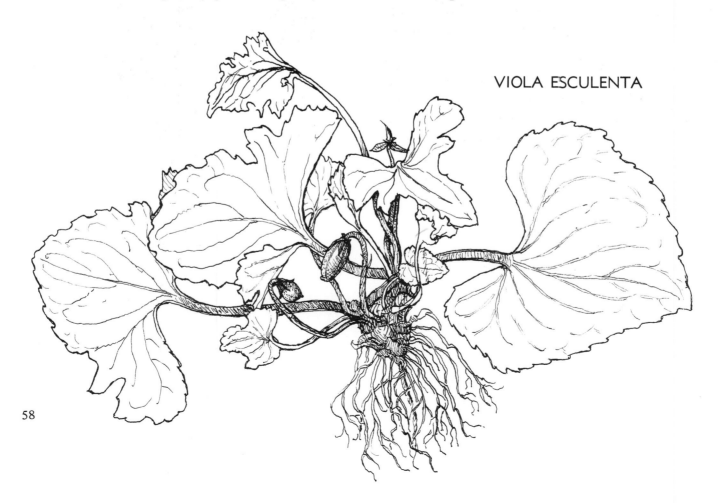

VIOLA ESCULENTA

VIOLA LOVELLIANA Brainerd

The Lovell Violet

Plates XXI, XXII

One cannot mistake this delightful southwestern violet, for even though the lobing of the leaves is somewhat similar to *V. sagittata,* there are too many distinguishing differences.

The flowers of *V. Lovelliana* are larger than those of *V. sagittata* and grow on long slender pedicels held noticeably high above the leaves. The early growth on stipules, back of leaves, and tops of petioles is softly pubescent on *V. Lovelliana,* while the summer appearance is entirely different on the two plants. *V. sagittata* grows very tall with large leaves on long petioles, while *V. Lovelliana,* though it stretches out somewhat, remains small. In addition, the leaves of *V. Lovelliana* take on a very firm, smooth quality as they age, gradually assuming reddish-brown, autumn coloring.

V. Lovelliana is found in shady hardwood or pine forests from North Carolina to Florida and west to Oklahoma. The plants shown on Plate XXI came from Florida; the flowering plants on Plate XXII were sent to me from Texas, and arrived in full bloom toward the end of March. They are a warm lavender-violet, usually darker toward the center, the outside of the petals paler, and the buds appearing white. The cleistogenes are at first on prostrate peduncles usually buried in the soil; the capsules are large and may be dotted purple.

Planted in appropriate woods this violet should thrive farther north.

GROUP II

STEMLESS BLUE
CUT-LEAVED

Violas pedata
       pedatifida
       septemloba
       Brittoniana
       Egglestonii
       viarum
       triloba dilitata
       triloba
       palmata
       Stoneana

VIOLA PEDATA L.

The Bird's-foot Violet

Plates XXIII, XXIV

This gorgeous violet is unmistakable. There are two forms: the all lavender or lilac, formerly called *"lineariloba,"* and its white form; and the bi-color, usually rich velvety purple on the two upper petals and lavender, lilac, or white on the lower petals. There are many variations, especially in southern stands, such as the upper drawing in Plate XXIII, from Georgia, and the lower one from a slide from West Virginia.

Characteristics of *Viola pedata* are: a thick upright rootstock, beautifully cut leaves; large, flat, open flowers; no cleistogenes; and often a second blooming in fall.

It is widespread throughout the east, both north and south, and as far west as Wisconsin. It may be found in full sun or half-shade along roadside banks at the edge of woods, in pine duff on the shore of a pond, in pine or other acid-woodland conditions, or even on railroad embankments. What it must have is good soil rich in humus, good drainage, and most important, an acid reaction in the soil. I was never successful with it until I added iron chelates to my neutral soil to acidify it. This comes as a crystal, often under a trade name, but will say "chelates of iron" on the label. With plenty of peat, sand and stone chips in the soil, and sun for part of the day, the plants respond and show their needs are being met by giving their usual long second blooming in the fall.

Increasing *pedata* plants has always been a problem. They do not set seed readily, a single plant cannot be divided, and ordinary cuttings do not work. Now it has been found that cuttings can be successfully taken. In the October 1965 *Bulletin of The American Rock Garden Society* two methods were described: either taking vertical divisions of the "carrot" with some leafage and root attached, in winter, and growing on in a greenhouse, or taking similar cuttings in April and growing on in a coldframe. In the July 1967 issue of the same bulletin a successful method of taking typical root cuttings was described.

VIOLA PEDATIFIDA Don G.

Larkspur Violet or Purple Prairie Violet

Plate XXV

This is another beautiful, cut-leaved violet, but it is not so fussy as is *V. pedata*. The plants that are illustrated came from South Dakota. In addition to the Dakotas it is found in Montana, New Mexico, Oklahoma, and Arizona. Claude Barr, who sent them to me, said that the one in seed was about half the normal size because of the drought. It looked larger to me than any I had previously seen.

When the leaves come up in spring they might possibly be mistaken for *V. pedata,* but as the plants develop, differences are obvious. The showy flowers are a different shape, of a soft red-violet veined darker. They are bearded as *V. pedata* is not, and never have *pedata's* two-toned form. The flowers are carried well above the leaves and the cleistogenes (never seen in *V. pedata*) are on short erect peduncles, growing taller as they ripen. The long-blooming period reaches from April to June.

The rootstock of *V. pedatifida* is not as long nor so heavy as that of *V. pedata*. Also, the leaves of *V. pedatifida* have more divisions, more prominent veins, and sometimes short, stiff hairs on the margins of the leaves and on the veins on the back of the leaves—all points of difference.

Though it is usually found in dry, open plains, the plant responds to well-drained moisture in gardens and presents no great difficulty in cultivation. During wet seasons in its native habitat it may grow to ten inches high, but in eastern gardens it is more likely to be half that size.

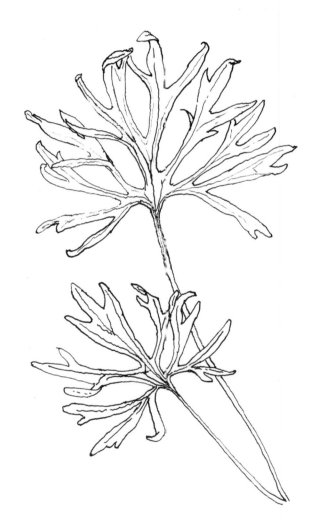

VIOLA PEDATIFIDA

Plate XX

VIOLA ESCULENTA

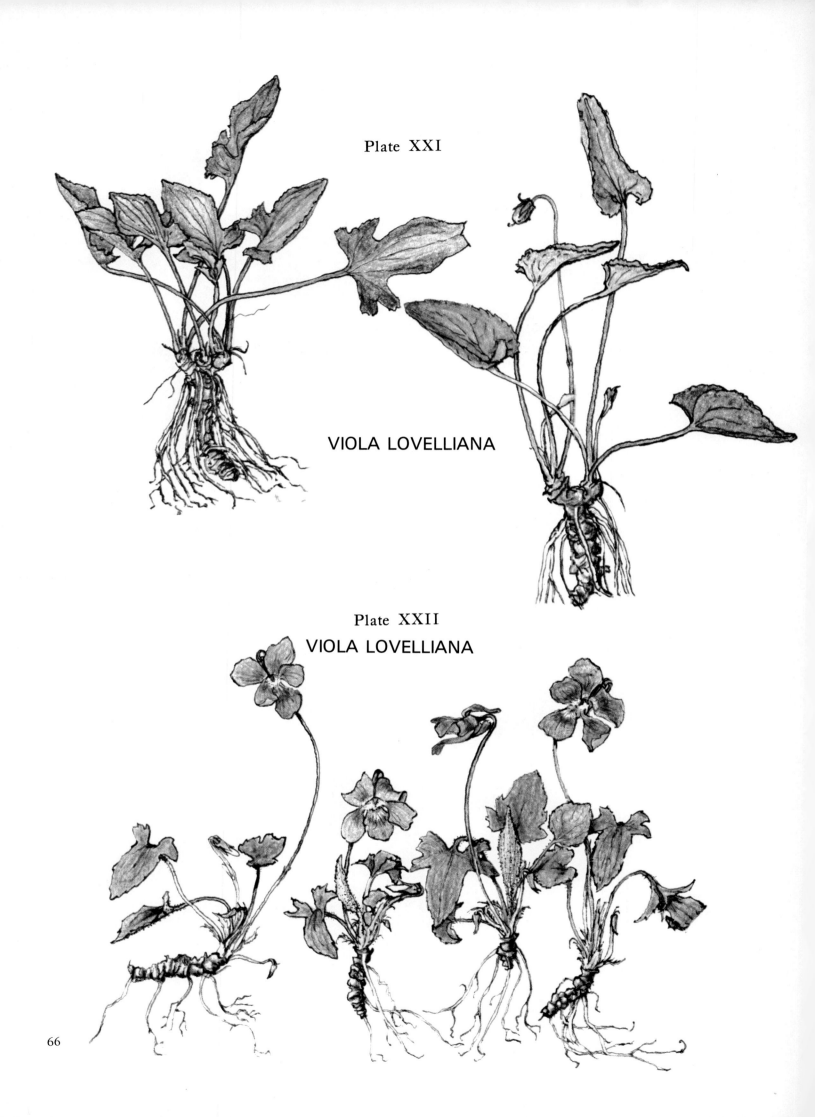

Plate XXI

VIOLA LOVELLIANA

Plate XXII

VIOLA LOVELLIANA

66

Plate XXIII

VIOLA PEDATA

Plate XXIV

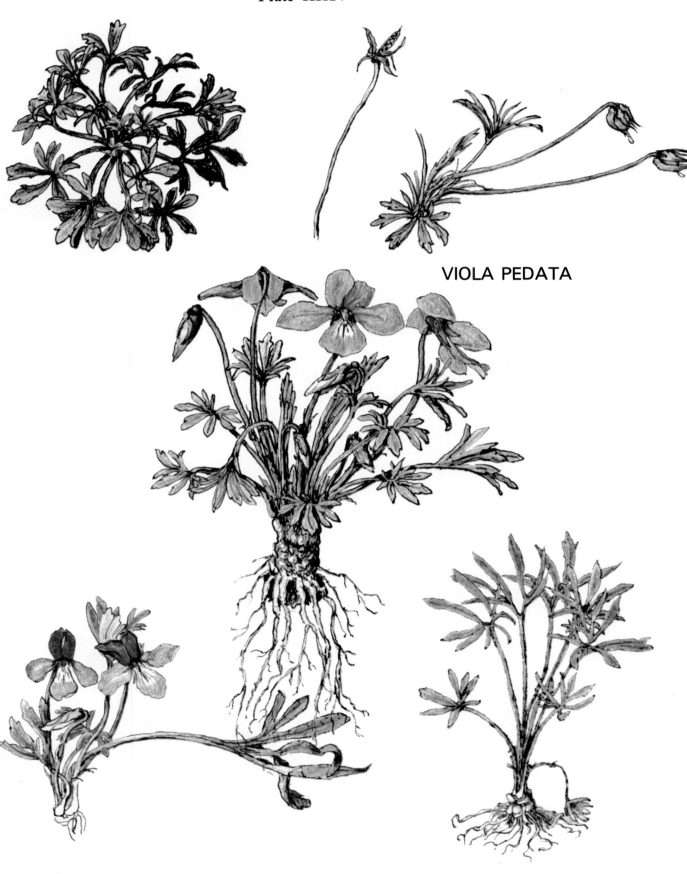

VIOLA PEDATA

Plate XXV

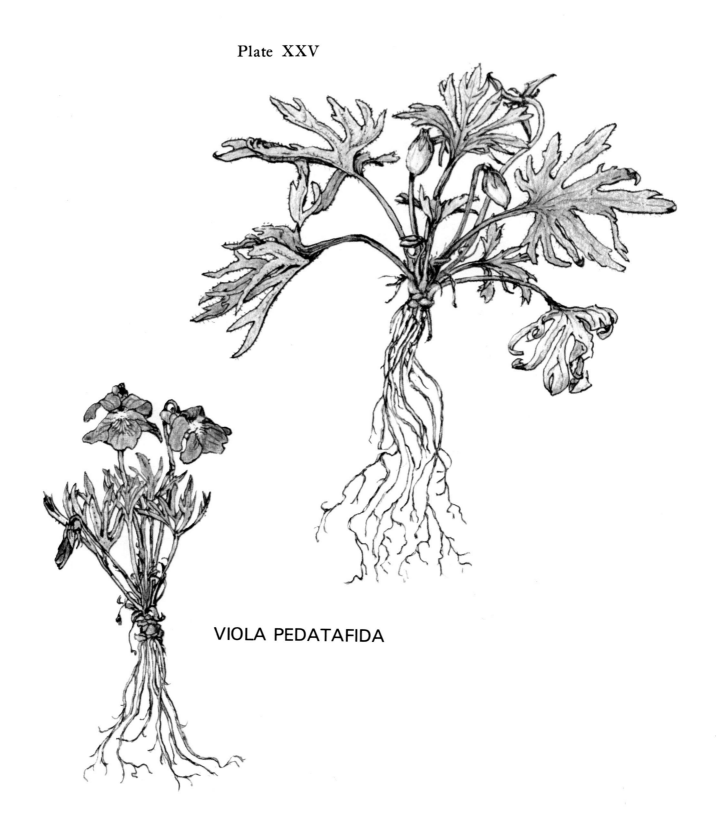

VIOLA PEDATAFIDA

Plate XXVI

VIOLA SEPTEMLOBA

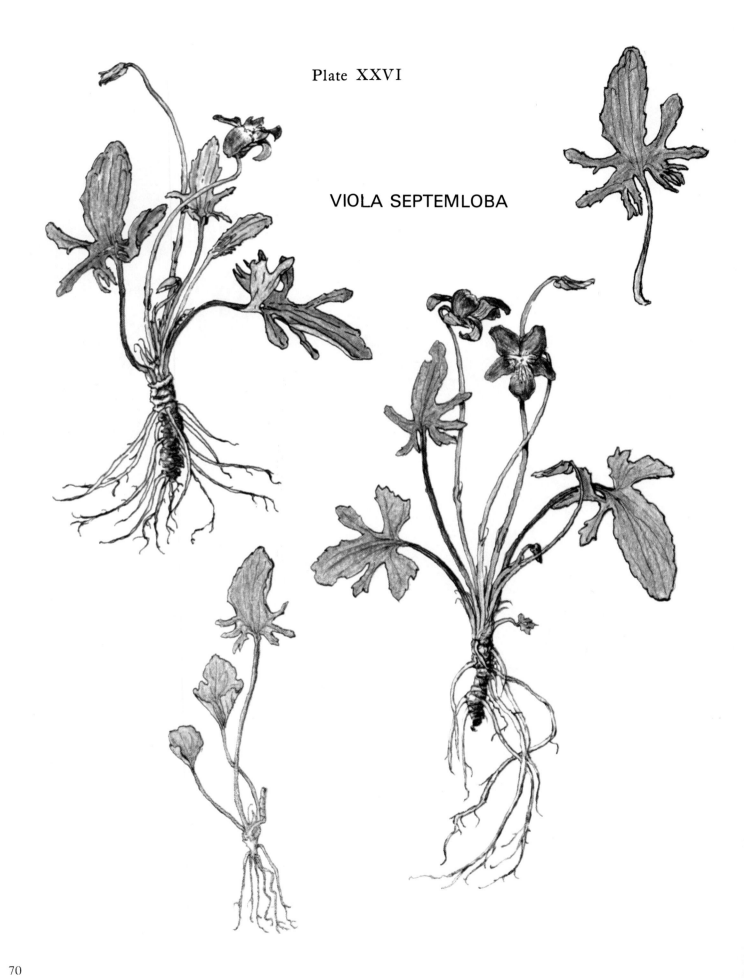

Plate XXVII

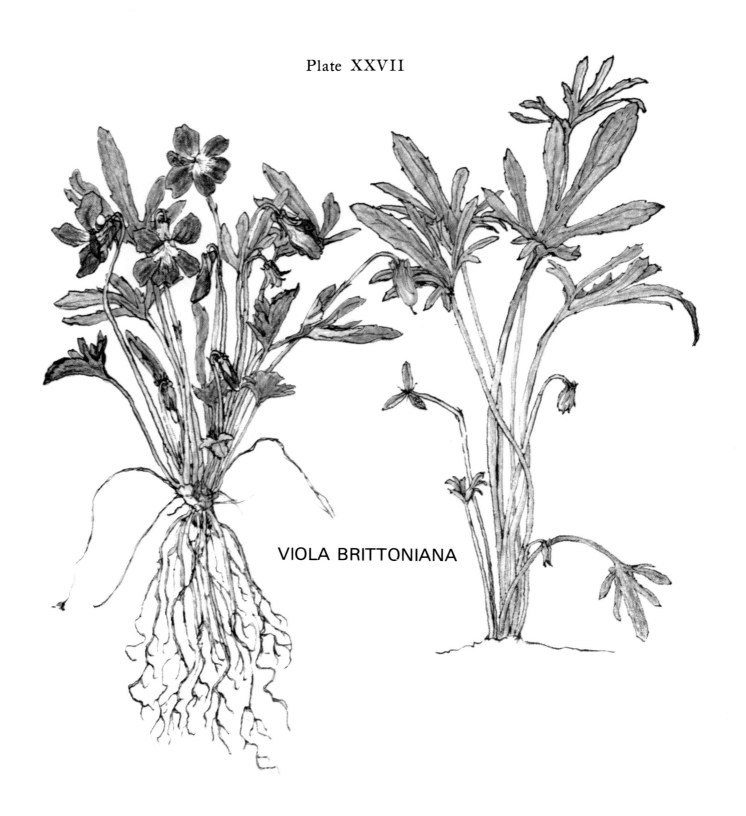

VIOLA BRITTONIANA

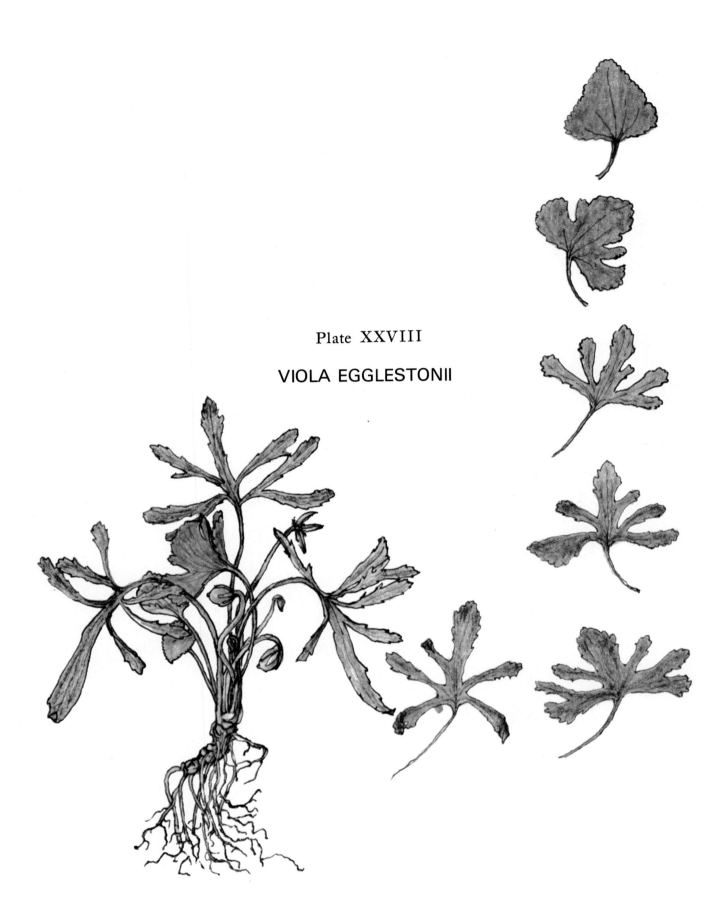

Plate XXVIII

VIOLA EGGLESTONII

Plate XXIX

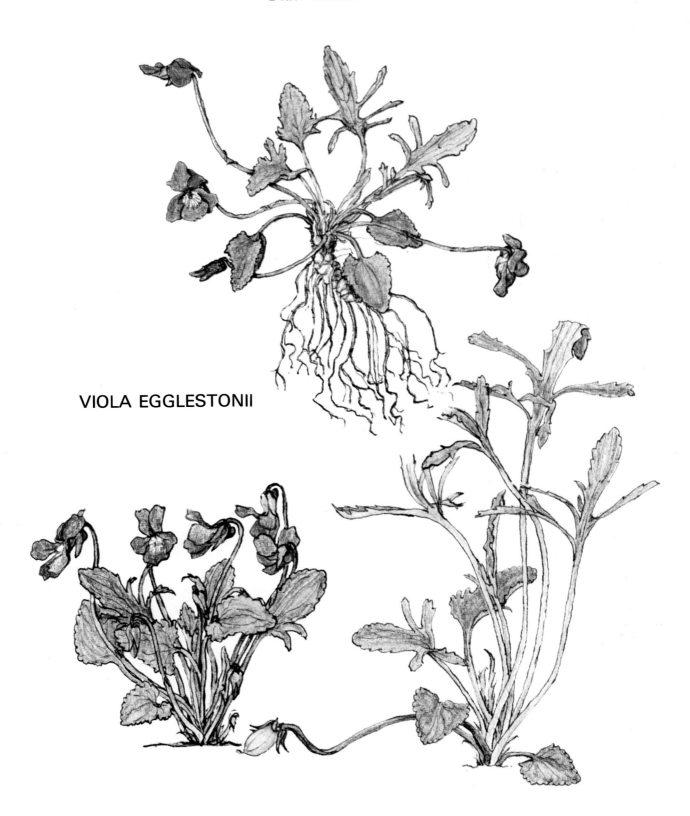

VIOLA EGGLESTONII

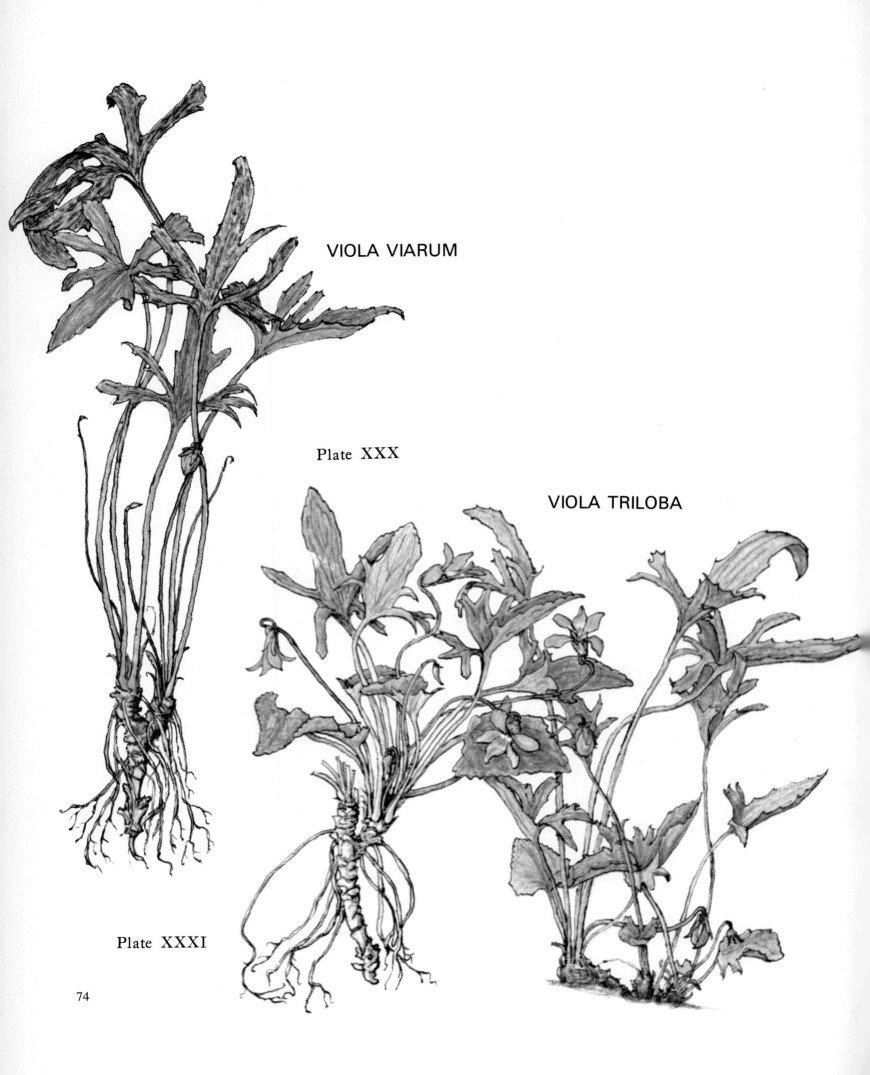

VIOLA VIARUM

Plate XXX

VIOLA TRILOBA

Plate XXXI

74

Plate XXXII

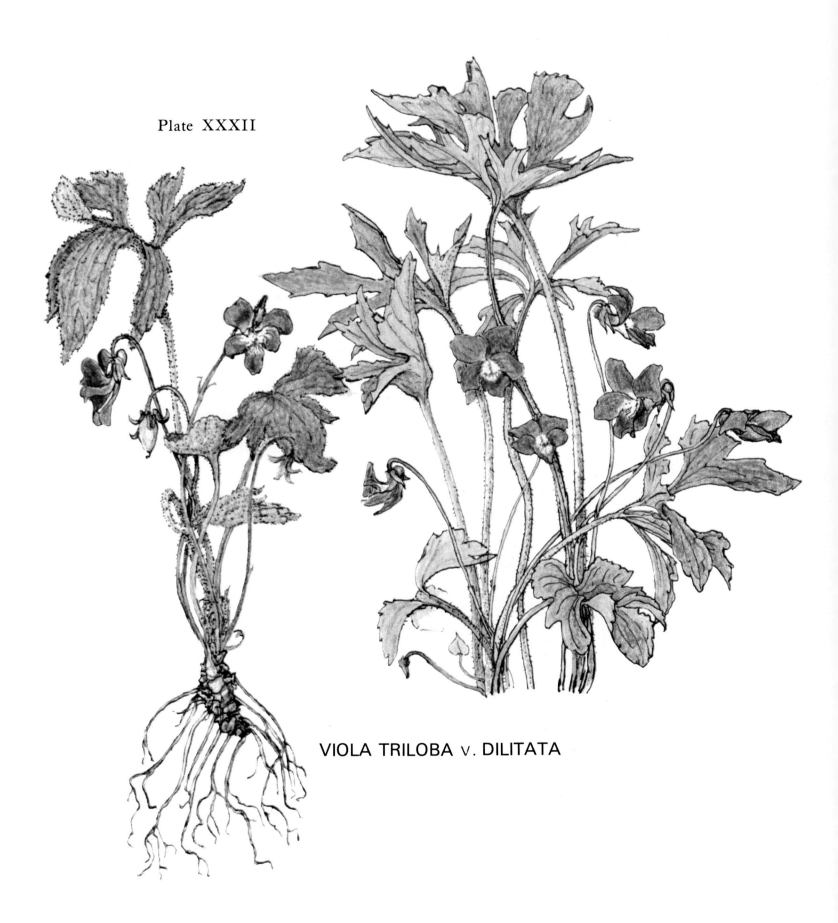

VIOLA TRILOBA v. DILITATA

Plate XXXIII

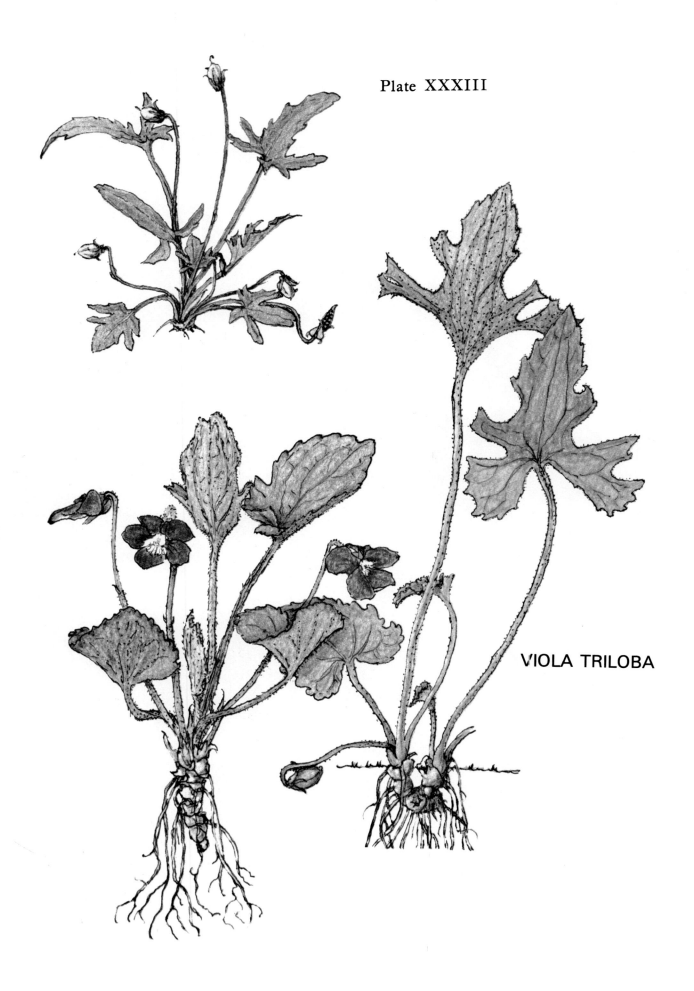

VIOLA TRILOBA

Plate XXIV

VIOLA TRILOBA

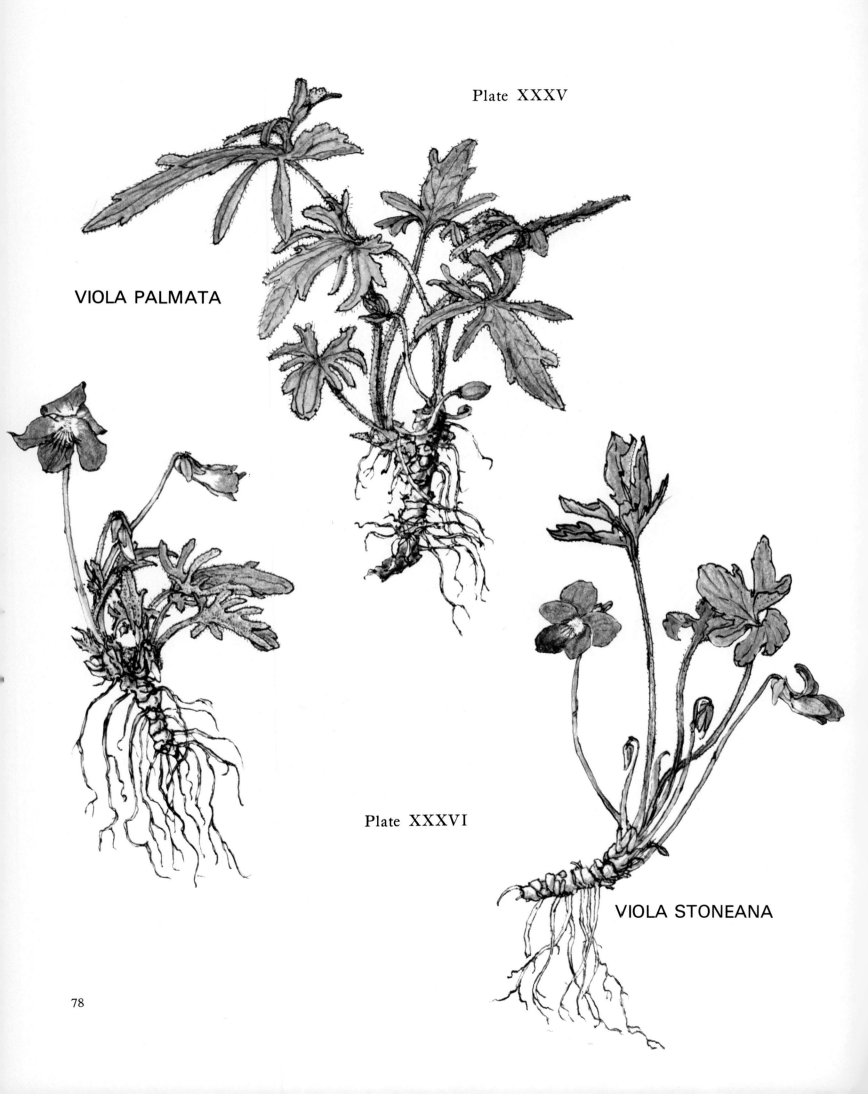

Plate XXXV

VIOLA PALMATA

Plate XXXVI

VIOLA STONEANA

Plate XXXVII

VIOLA STONEANA

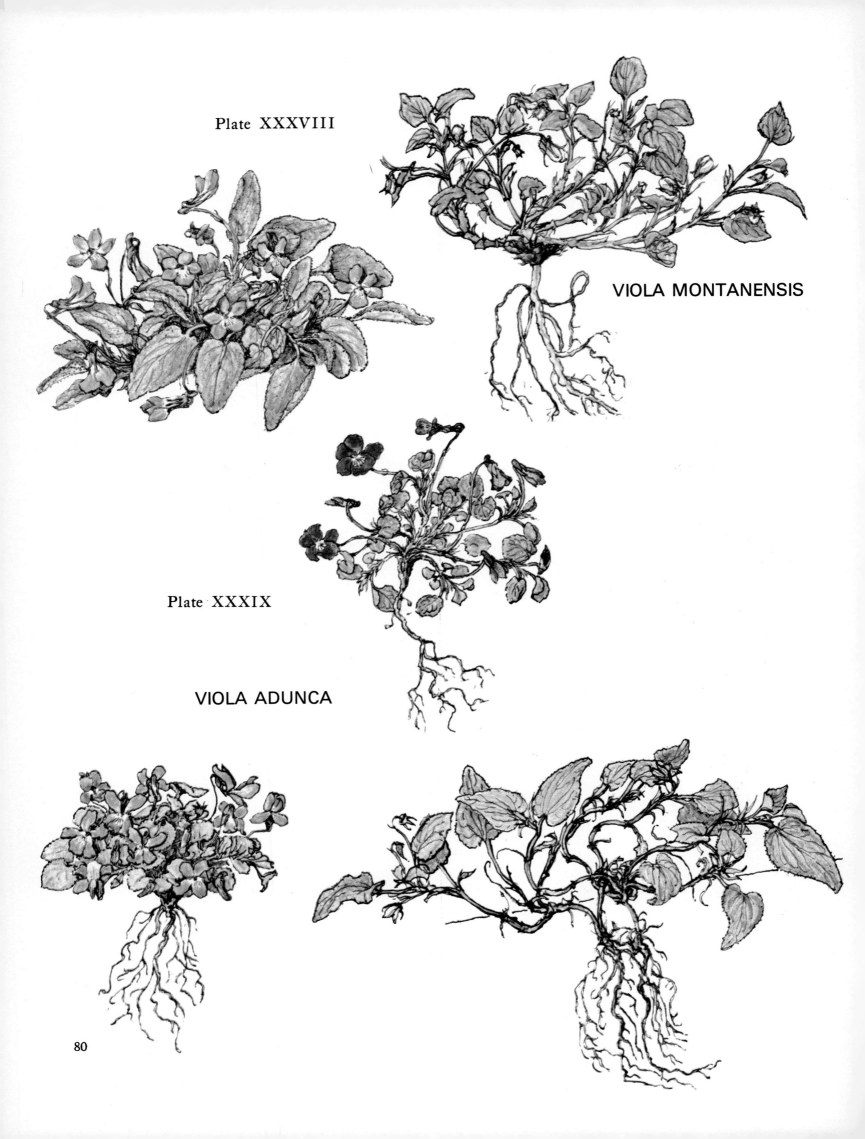

Plate XXXVIII

VIOLA MONTANENSIS

Plate XXXIX

VIOLA ADUNCA

80

VIOLA SEPTEMLOBA Le Conte

The Southern Coastal Violet

Plate XXVI

From the rather dry pine barrens of southeastern Virginia, Florida, and west to Mississippi, comes this attractive member of the clan. Those on Plate XXVI came from Florida.

The large flowers are a showy red-violet on long peduncles over-topping the leaves, with the three

VIOLA SEPTEMLOBA

lower petals white at the base and heavily bearded, with dark-purple lines. The cleistogenes grow erect.

The leaves are most variable, not always showing "seven" lobes, and are sometimes entire on young foliage. It might be confused with *Viola Brittoniana* (see Plate XXVII), but if you will compare the drawings you will see that the lobing is different; *V. septemloba* has a heavier central lobe and its lower lobes point downward. The flowers are a different shape in the two plants and there are evident differences in the root systems and general appearance.

I received one plant of *V. septemloba* from Florida, from Dorcas Brigham, which was much taller with larger paler flowers than the one shown. She told me that it had grown so tall because where it was found it was growing in competition with grasses and other wildflowers. So you see how difficult it is to lay down the law about any of these violets. It's like a class of children. On the first day of school they all look much alike to the teacher, but very soon different personalities develop, and with familiarity she soon knows one from the other.

In gardens *V. septemloba* needs light shade in a humus-filled, acid soil. Where pine needles are not available, you might have to resort to a generous use of peat and sand, or perhaps the addition of iron chelates to the soil.

VIOLA BRITTONIANA Pollard

Britton's or the Sand Violet

Plate XXVII

In the eastern part of the country from Maine to Virginia and to North Carolina, *Viola Brittoniana* will be found in moist, rich, peaty, sandy soil, or in grassy positions. Those on Plate XXVII were collected for me in New Jersey. While at first glance so many of these cut-leaved blue violets look much alike, you will know this one by its *smooth,* rather regularly and finely cut leaves, which in early spring are reddish underneath. There is a form called *V. pectinata* that is sometimes found growing with the cut-leaved form, and has rather long triangular leaves with deep crenations near the base.

The flowers are large and striking—usually of a bright reddish-violet, even with or just exceeding the leaves in height—with pronounced white beards and light centers. If you compare them with the other "blue" flowers in this group you will note differences in size, shape, and color. They bloom in May and June. Their pale-green cleistogenes grow on upright stalks.

This beauty should do well in rock gardens where the soil would probably suit its needs, in sun where it is moist, in more shade where it is dryer.

VIOLA BRITTONIANA

VIOLA EGGLESTONII Brainerd

The Tennessee Violet

Plates XXVIII, XXIX

When I read that *Viola Egglestonii* came from only one section of the country, Central Tennessee, I wondered how I was going to secure any. Then one day a friend, Cleo Fitch, showed up and said she was going down to visit Nashville, her hometown. That was also the home of *Viola Egglestonii* —an exciting coincidence—and I begged her to try to find it for me. She did, and it arrived in excellent condition. What a thrill!

Cleo wrote me: "They were growing on the side of a country road in sun, on the south side of a cedar barren in about an inch of soil. The roots ran down into crevices of limestone. A cedar barren has the thinnest layer of lichens and mosses over limestone strata. The plants were scattered about a foot apart."

The deeply cut, brownish leaves on the plant shown here were on their way out, which seems to be usual in fall. I drew a number of the other leaves to show their great variation—from entire to variously cut forms.

They were not in bloom when received, so I planted them in a cold-frame in semi-shade, adding no lime to my neutral or slightly acid soil, and placing small stones around them to protect the roots over winter. The opposite plate shows what came up in spring. Dr. Ben Channel of Vanderbilt University at Nashville checked my drawings for accuracy and sent me additional plants.

VIOLA VIARUM Pollard

The Plains Violet

Plate XXX

Viola viarum is widely distributed in the midwest. The plant shown came from Michigan. It comes from either moist but well-drained positions, such as riverbanks and flood-plain forests, or else rather dry positions, such as railroad banks, and will grow in either sun or shade. Dr. Russell considers it a member of the *affinis-missouriensis* complex, and believes it may be only a form of *V. missouriensis* rather than a separate species.

As you can see on the picture of *V. missouriensis* (Plate V) in Group I, the uncut leaf of *V. viarum* is almost identical with one on *V. missouriensis*.

The rootstock too is rather similar, *V. missouriensis* often branching as does the one shown on *V. viarum*.

The petal shapes shown on *V. viarum* are characteristic (although the color may vary to a deeper violet): the rather tubular inrolling spur petal, the narrow (bearded) laterals converging about the spurred petal, and the broader, divergent, upper petals.

There should be no difficulty in cultivating *V. viarum* in any reasonable position.

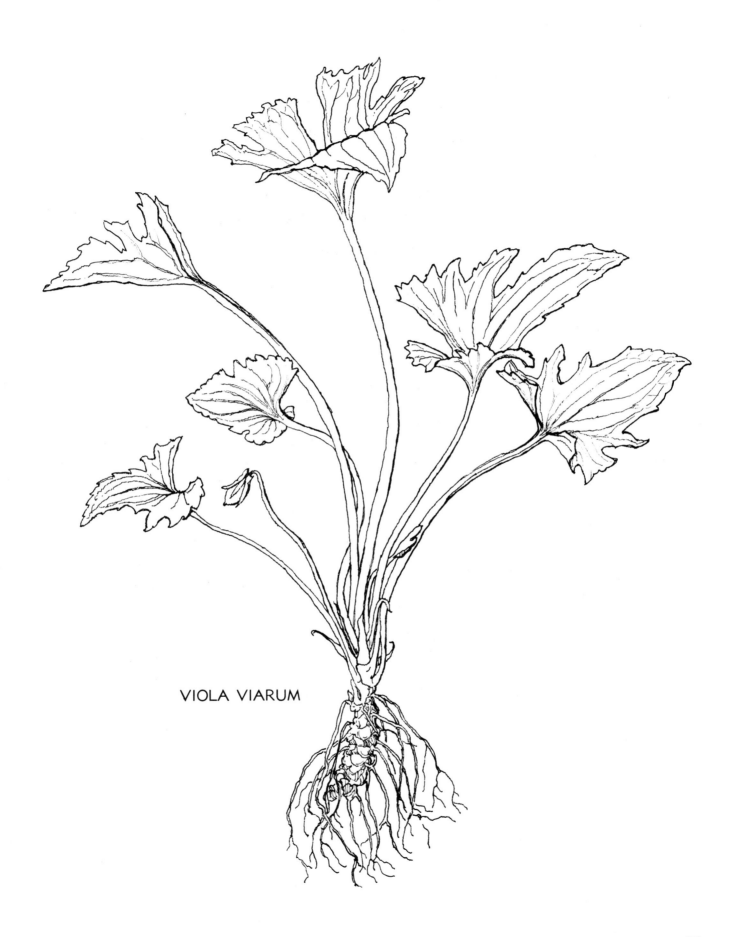

VIOLA VIARUM

VIOLA TRILOBA var. DILITATA Bra nerd

Cut-leaved Triloba

VIOLA TRILOBA Schwein.

Three-parted Triloba

Plates XXXI, XXXII, XXXIII, XXXIV

Plates XXXI and XXXII show several forms of the deeply cut *V. triloba* var. *dilitata* which are much more deeply cut than the species, *V. triloba,* shown on the two following Plates XXXIII and XXXIV. Russell says that the type is more characteristic of the Appalachians and that *V. dilitata* occurs at and beyond the fringes of the former. The rather woolly plant on Plate XXXII came from Texas, while the two other drawings were made from Pennsylvania plants.

V. triloba caused me a great deal of confusion, largely I think because I raised it from seed. New seedlings frequently do not show the deeply lobed leaves that are typical of the plant later on, but my main trouble was that the seeds were labeled "palmata." The confusion is not unnatural, for all these violets hybridize with one another and one may get one of the betwixt and between when raising them from seed, and *V. palmata* and *V. triloba* have many similarities.

The plants, very low at first, are larger at flowering time and still larger as they go to seed—a trap for the unwary. The small buds are cleistogamous flowers which develop into fat pods that seed prolifically and spread quickly. Further, there is considerable variation in the color of the flowers, which are often spoken of as "blue."

V. triloba is found over a large part of the eastern United States, frequently in dry woods, such as our own hillside, where the hairy ones on Plate XXXIII were found.

V. triloba as well as *V. dilitata* seem to adapt to varying types of soil and varying amounts of shade. One has to watch so that this violet does not colonize where it is not wanted.

86

VIOLA PALMATA L.

The Palmate Violet

Plate XXXV

Viola palmata is widespread from Massachusetts west to the Great Lakes and Minnesota, and from the Appalachians to north Georgia and other south Atlantic states. There is the usual variation in the appearance of the plants, but one should be able to recognize their deeply cut leaves, hairy on the under surface, edges, and petioles; purple flowers that overtop the leaves; their heavy rootstock; prostrate cleistogenes on short pedicels.

My first sight of *Viola palmata* surprised me. It was collected in New York. It was not in bloom and its large leaves were about eight inches high and so very hairy—a most unviolet-like plant. In the south the plants can be almost glabrous. Though considered close to *V. Egglestonii* (Plates XXVIII and XXIX), it is so much larger and heavier that the two can hardly be confused. Like most violets it hybridizes with neighboring members of the clan.

The large, violet-colored flowers, which can vary somewhat in color, have white centers heavily bearded. They can be found in bloom in April and May.

Because *V. palmata* comes from rich, dry woods, it needs some similar position to thrive, and may disappear if planted in too moist a location.

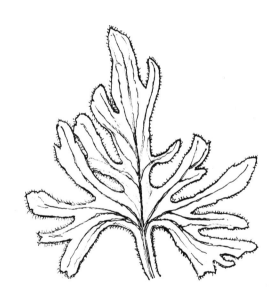

VIOLA PALMATA

VIOLA STONEANA House

Stone's Violet

Plates XXXVI, XXXVII

Viola Stoneana, long considered a species close to *V. palmata,* is now placed among the hybrids. This plant was collected in Pennsylvania.

As one can see by comparing it with *V. palmata* (Plate XXXV) the leaves are not too dissimilar, and *Viola Stoneana,* while hairy, is less so than *V. palmata.* Root system, cleistogenes and buds are all close to each other. Also, the later leaves of *V. palmata* are frequently larger and heavier than those shown on Plate XXXV.

Other cut-leaved violets may be found near quite different species in different localities, but on examination, if not found to be one of the definite species, they will probably show similarities to the violets among which they are growing.

To quote Russell on this subject, "One expects a species to be somewhat consistent in its appearance and to have a rather definite geographic range. Neither is true of *Stoneana."*

V. Stoneana is an example of a beautiful violet that might be mistaken for a species, but is actually one of the hybrids that violets produce so freely.

GROUP III

STEMMED BLUE
UNCUT*

Violas montanensis
        adunca
        Walteri
        appalachiensis
        conspersa
        labradorica
        Howellii
        rostrata
        palustris
        epipsela
        Selkirkii
        Flettii
        tricolor
        odorata
        western odorata

* The stem of the "stemmed" violet is evident, with leaves and flowers branching from it, except:
1. As you glance at it on the ground, you may see only a cluster of leaves with the flowers growing from them. This is usually the early spring condition. If you look closely you will see the stems spraying from a central cluster of leaves. As the season advances, many of these violets, such as *V. conspersa* and *V. striata,* grow taller and taller until you can easily see a whole forest of stems up to 12 to 15 inches long.
2. The seedlings of stemmed violets usually do not show stems in their early stage.

VIOLA MONTANENSIS Rydb.

The Montana Violet

Plate XXXVIII

Although Dr. Russell considers *V. montanensis* a form of *V. adunca*, I show it here as a member of a complex of closely related species. To a gardener it has enough distinction to seem to warrant a Plate of its own. The other species of the complex are: *Violas adunca, appalachiensis, Walteri, labradorica, conspersa, rostrata,* and *Howellii*. These will be found on the Plates following this one.

V. montanensis is a softer, more pubescent plant than *V. adunca* and, while it is a stemmed species, the stems at first are very short and hold it in a tight clump rather than spreading as in most of the *aduncas*. Normally the flowers of *V. montanensis* are paler in color than those of *V. adunca* and its leaves are usually longer and narrower.

Claude Barr, who sent me the plant and wrote the above details to me from South Dakota, says, "give it more or less shade, very good soil and better than average moisture."

VIOLA ADUNCA J. E. Smith

Western Dog-Violet, Hooked-spur Violet

Plates XXXIX, XL

Neither of the common names of *V. adunca* is exact, as it grows both east and west across the northern party of the country, and the spurs may be either hooked or straight. It is usually found in open, dry habitats, though it will grow elsewhere. It has so many variations in size and color that a number of the different forms are shown. The large plant on Plate XXXIX is the least typical (though I have received large forms from both New York and Montana) but shows what a swampy condition can do. The small flowering plant on Plate XL is a cultivated form drawn from a slide from Alaska; the *bellidifolia* form is usually found in mountain areas, while the little plant at the foot of the page came from a Connecticut dooryard. The other drawings show various forms as they developed.

You just have to know that *V. adunca* is a stemmed species, although the stem may be very short; it is some shade of violet with a white center and bearded lateral petals, a slender rootstock, leaves slightly cordate or truncate, and flowers carried well above the leaves.

Naturally, a species that grows in such varied habitats and assumes so many forms adapts readily to many differing environments.

VIOLA WALTERI House

Walter's Violet or
Prostrate Southern Violet

Plate XLI

This "rare and adorable violet," as Elizabeth Lawrence wrote of it, is distinctly southern, widespread but not prolific through West Virginia, Maryland, Florida, Georgia and Texas. It is found in rich acid-soil forests in shade or half-shade, and its associates may be *Violas villosa* and *Lovelliana*. Dr. Edgar T. Wherry says he has seen it in such positions where it will make two-foot mats and can be recognized from a distance by a glow given off by the leaves. On close examination under a magnifying glass the leaves seem to be sprinkled with stardust, but if you increase the magnification you can see that these are really the tiniest of white hairs that shine in the light—a pubescence that covers the surface and edges of the leaves—but to the naked eye just gives them a silvery appearance. *V. Walteri* spreads by runners that root and form new, detachable plants. The upper plant came from Texas, in bloom in March; the central plants on Plate XLI from a station in Virginia, its most northerly position. The plant at the bottom of the page was sent from North Carolina.

V. Walteri can be found in bloom in March and April. Its delicate lavender flowers with white centers, dark lines and bearded laterals, are held above the leaves. In early spring the stem is not very evident, but it soon elongates and ascends—then inclines. The cleistogenes grow in the axils of the leaves along the stems, capsules green to red-purple.

In the north it might be safest to grow it on a shady slope among rocks in an acid-soil mixture, where it gets good drainage but adequate moisture —a perfect rock-garden plant.

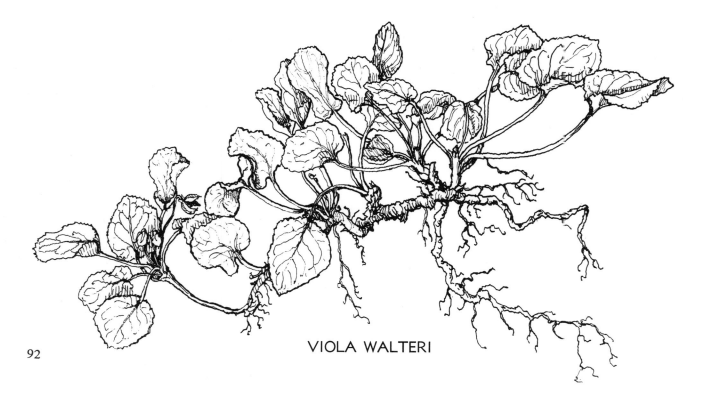

VIOLA WALTERI

VIOLA APPALACHIENSIS Henry

Appalachian Violet

Plates XLII, XLIII

This plant (and another named *V. alleghenien-sis*) is considered by Dr. Russell to be close to either *V. conspersa* (Plate XLIV) or *V. Walteri* bordering on *V. conspersa*. Wherry and some other botanists think that *V. appalachiensis* warrants specific treatment. I show it here because while it has the same manner of growth as *V. Walteri* and may well be a mountain form of that lowland violet, it is an interesting variation.

The leaves and whole plant are smaller than *V. Walteri* and appear more prostrate than *V. con-spersa,* but, of course, this would be natural in a mountain form. The color of the leaves of both *V. appalachiensis* and of *V. conspersa* is green, while *V. Walteri* has a certain amount of bronze in its coloring. Some forms of *V. appalachiensis* have fine pubescence on the edges and the surface of the leaves, but not enough to be noticeable at a distance as is true of *V. Walteri.* You can readily understand why these various violets are considered members of a complex.

As an example of what I'm talking about, on Plate XLII I show a darling seedling that came up in my garden. It is undoubtedly an early stage of one of the stemmed blue violets with uncut leaves. But which one? I was given a small plant labeled "dwarf *V. conspersa"* which this may be, but it has more bronze in the coloring of the leaves than either *V. conspersa* or *V. appalachiensis,* nearer *V. Walteri* or *V. labradorica.* You name it!

In half shade in woodland soil there is no problem in cultivating *V. appalachiensis.* It can also be grown in a partly shaded position in a rock-garden with plenty of humus in the soil.

VIOLA CONSPERSA Reichenb.

The Dog Violet

Plate XLIV

Although the blue, stemmed violets that we are considering have so much in common, *Viola conspersa* calls attention to itself by its color. It is not violet but light blue, though when you compare it to the pure blue of a forget-me-not, you can see that there is some lavender in it. It is one of the most common species of the central and northeastern United States.

I show three flowering plants, all blooming at the same time in my garden, on the edge of the woods where they get filtered sunlight. The tallest plant is in heavy matted growth and has reached up for the light; the smallest plant is a young one; the middle-sized plant is typical of those growing in open positions, with a three-inch spread and about that much showing above ground, usually a mass of blue.

The flowers rise from the axils of the stem-leaves, are striped darker and are lightly bearded. The small cleistogenes also rise from the axils of the leaves on the lengthening stems, as well as from the axils that bore the spring flowers. They continue to appear during the growing season.

In summer the long stems become prostrate, the leaves browning as they age, but leaving a cluster of small green leaves in the center of the plant.

A shaded or half-shaded position in good soil will insure healthy growth. I have never found *V. Conspersa* to be one of the pest group that seeds indiscriminately.

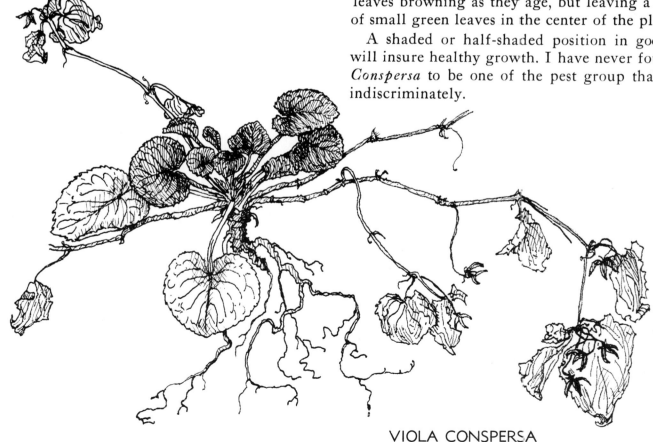

VIOLA CONSPERSA

VIOLA LABRADORICA Schrank

The Labrador Violet

Plate XLV

When I raised *Viola labradorica* from seed, I was intrigued by the very dark purple rosette of its early leaves. This color seems to characterize this violet, so that, at a glance, you can separate it from the other stemmed blue uncut violets, even though they all seem to show some purple coloring at one or another stage. Every description of this violet I have seen, has mentioned the "bronze" or "dark green with an overcast of metallic violet," or some such phrasing. On the other hand, the botanists all seem to describe it as being near or perhaps a subspecies of one of the other blue, stemmed violets. Dr. Russell considers it a smaller, northern replacement of *V. conspersa.*

It is found in only a few northern locations in this country, a bog near the shores of Lake Superior, Cook County in Minnesota, the White Mountains in New Hampshire, and Alaska.

It bloomed in May in my garden with deep lavender to violet flowers, white base and dark lines and bearded laterals. Most of the leaves showed some pubescence on the upper surface and were purplish underneath; the edges were evenly scalloped. On seedlings I found the flowers and leaves smaller and darker. The large flowering plant came from Connecticut. A fall flowering of smaller blossoms as shown in Plate XLV is not unusual.

As it is found in both bogs and woodland, rich, moist, well-drained soil is indicated with half-shade unless especially wet.

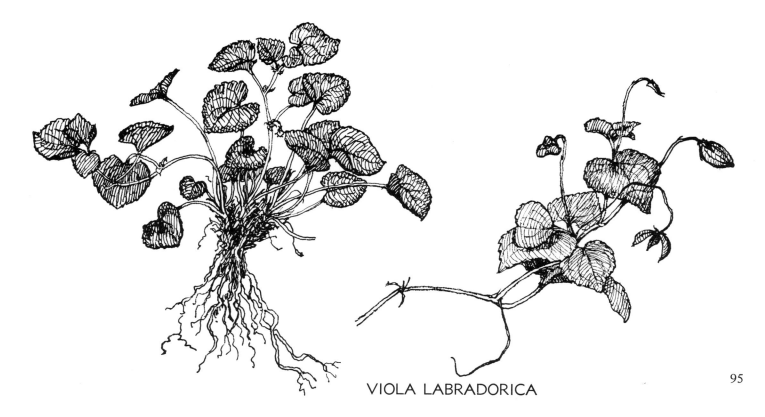

VIOLA LABRADORICA

95

VIOLA HOWELLII Gray

The Oregon Coastal Violet

Plate XLVI

There must be considerable variation in the color of *V. Howellii,* for the one sent me from Oregon has bright rose-madder color, but it is usually described as violet or soft blue and white, or blue-violet with white dark-lined base and bearded lateral petals. The flowers that surpass the leaves are as wide as they are long, giving them a roundish look. The spur is heavy and generally straight and the sepals show noticeable auricles. The cleistogenes are green and oblong.

Russell considers it one of the *adunca* complex, but we gardeners could hardly mistake it for any other, especially as *V. conspersa,* to which it seems nearest, is eastern and *V. Howellii* a westerner.

It can be either glabrous or sparsely pubescent; it has tall ascending stems and both leaves and flowers on long stalks. The leaves vary from a shallow sinus or a somewhat cuneate base to heart-shaped.

The plant is found in moist woods and meadows in Oregon and California. Ira N. Gabrielson writes of it in *Western American Alpines* as a woodlander from the Cascades and Coast Ranges. As it is deciduous, and thus gets some protection over the winter, it should thrive in other parts of the country in sun or half-shade.

Plate XL

VIOLA ADUNCA

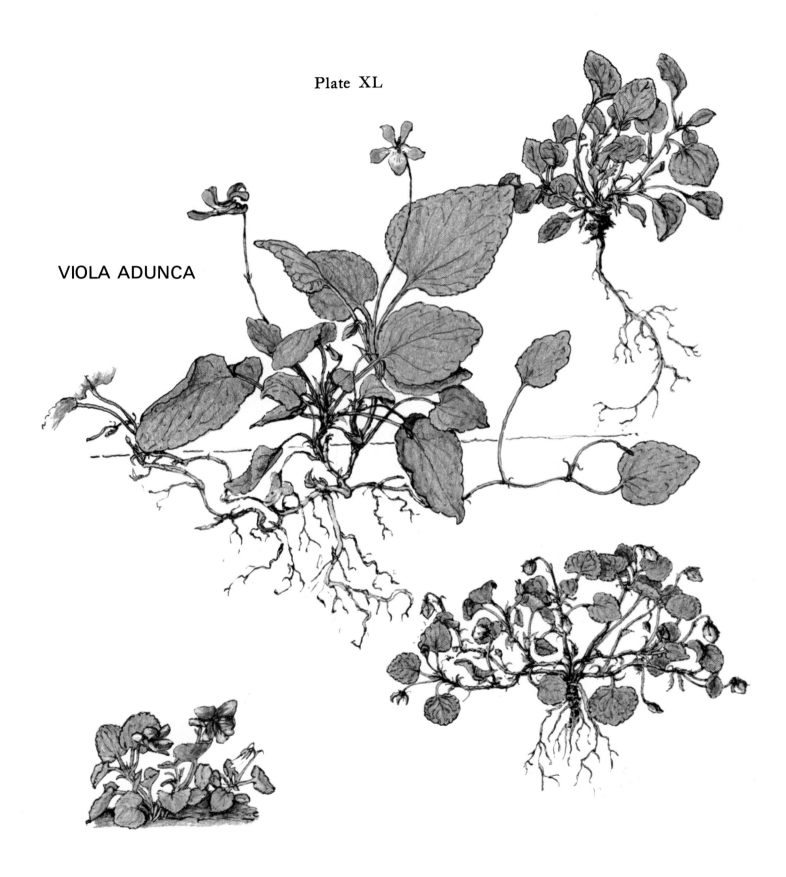

Plate XLI

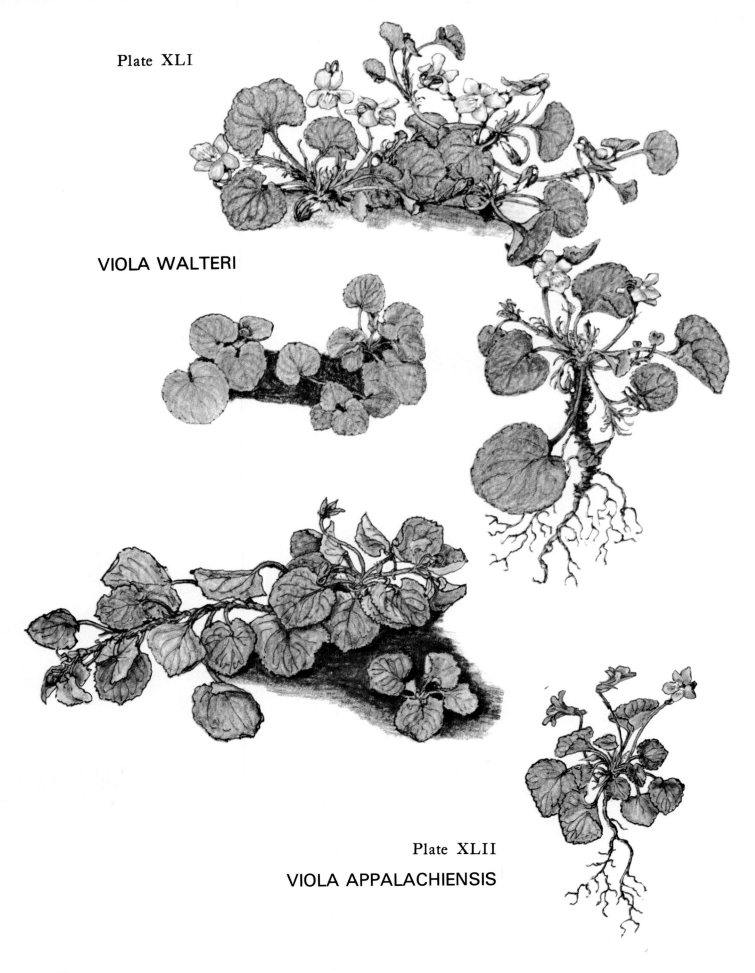

VIOLA WALTERI

Plate XLII

VIOLA APPALACHIENSIS

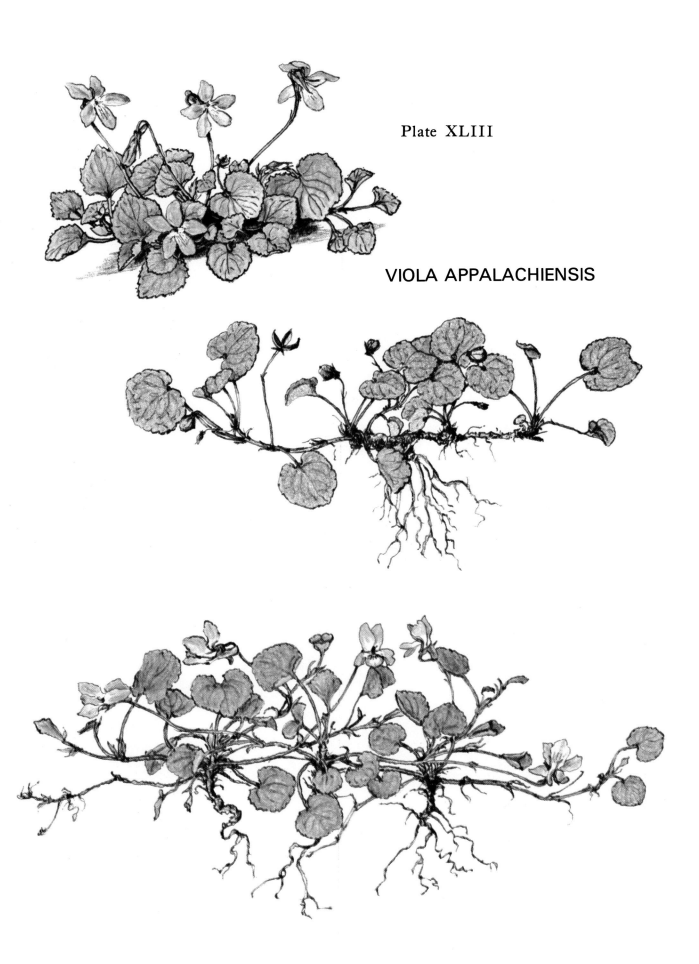

Plate XLIII

VIOLA APPALACHIENSIS

99

Plate XLIV

VIOLA CONSPERSA

Plate XLV

VIOLA LABRADORICA

Plate XLVI

VIOLA HOWELLII

Plate XLVII

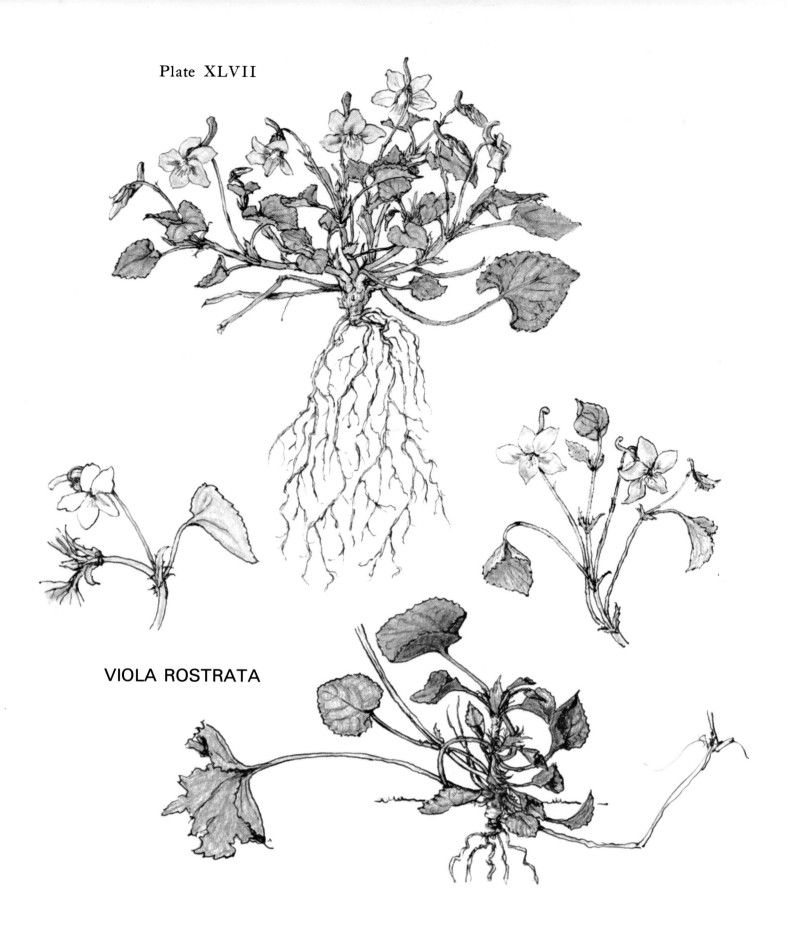

VIOLA ROSTRATA

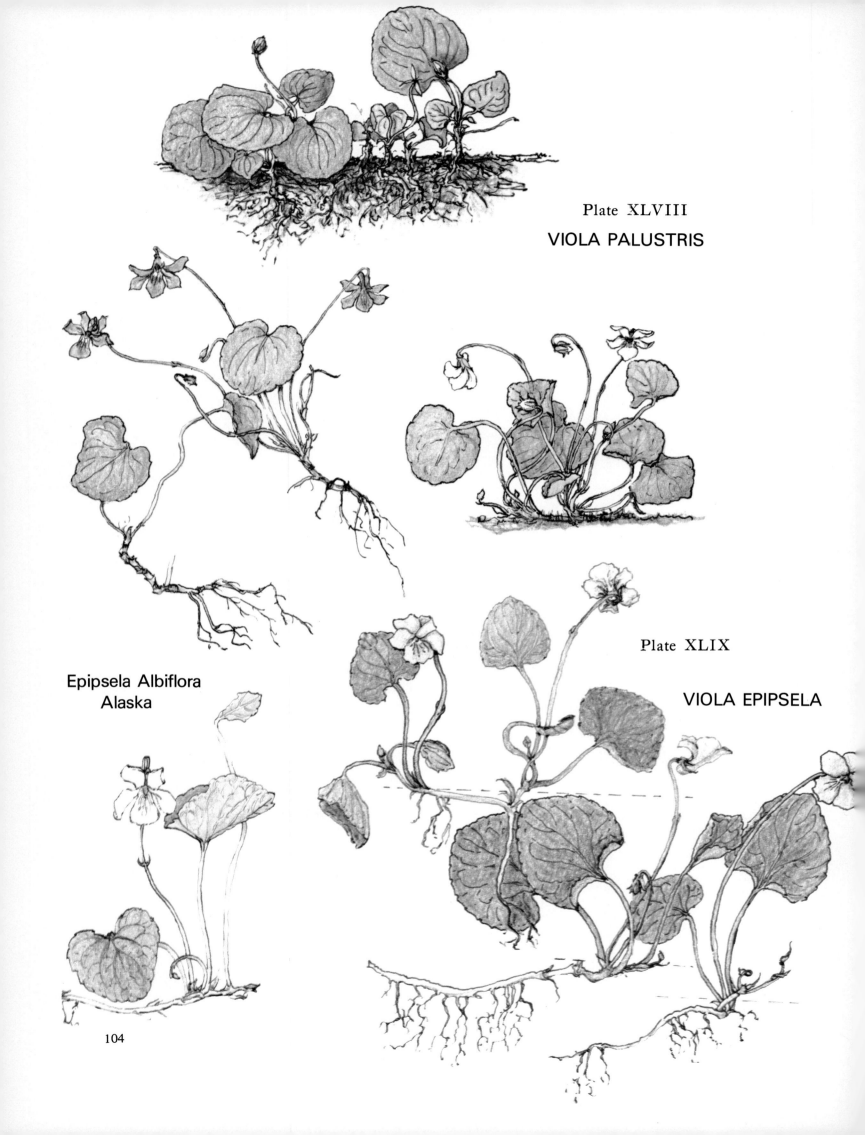

Plate XLVIII
VIOLA PALUSTRIS

Epipsela Albiflora
Alaska

Plate XLIX

VIOLA EPIPSELA

104

Plate L

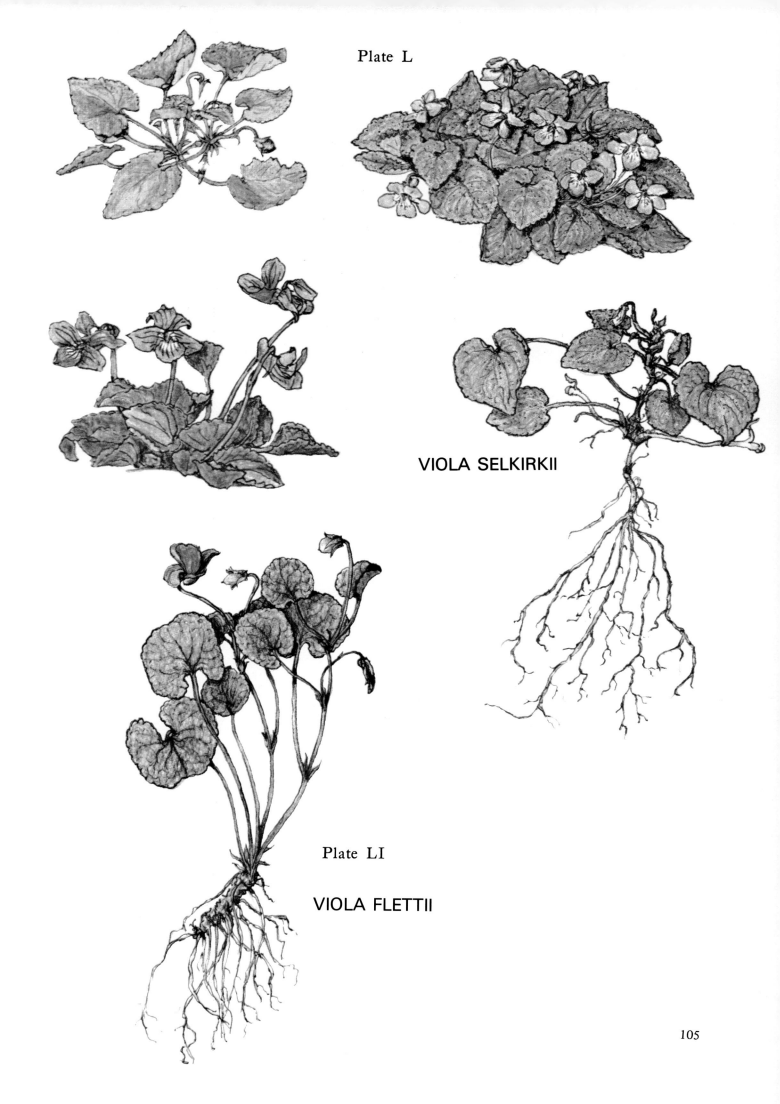

VIOLA SELKIRKII

Plate LI

VIOLA FLETTII

105

Plate LII

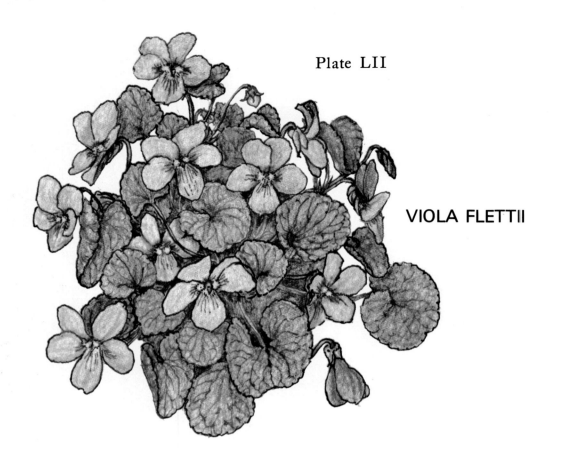

VIOLA FLETTII

Plate LIII

VIOLA TRICOLOR

Johnny-Jump-Up

Plate LIV

VIOLA TRICOLOR

Johnny-Jump-Up

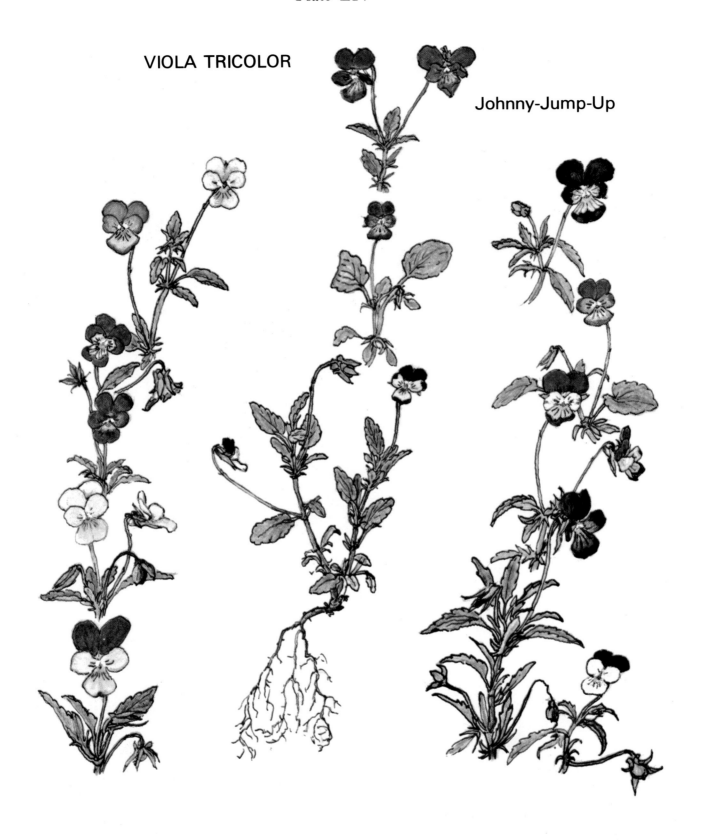

Plate LV

VIOLA ODORATA

Plate LVI

VIOLA ODORATA
(Western)

Plate LVII

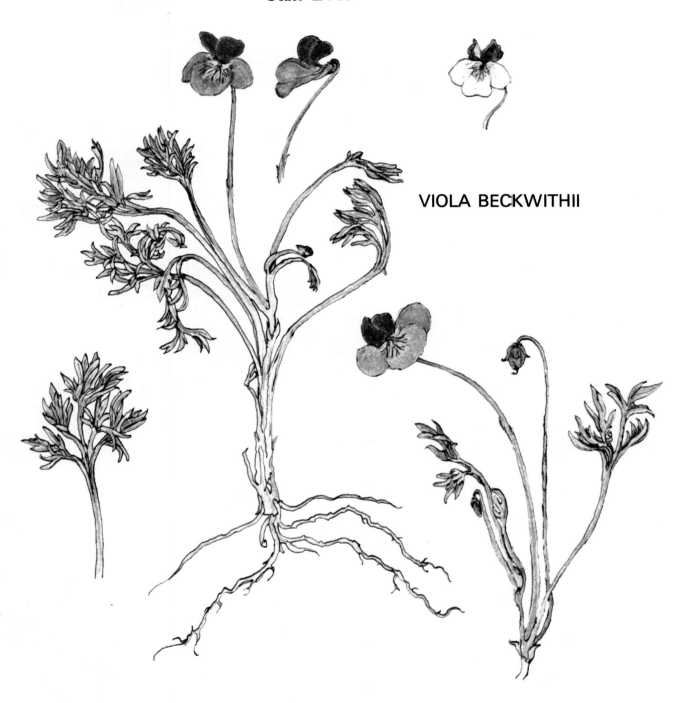

VIOLA BECKWITHII

Plate LVIII

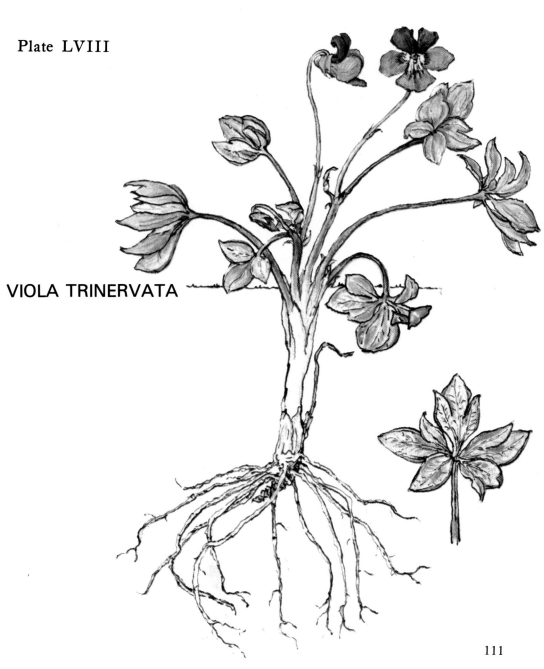

VIOLA TRINERVATA

Plate LIX

VIOLA TRINERVATA

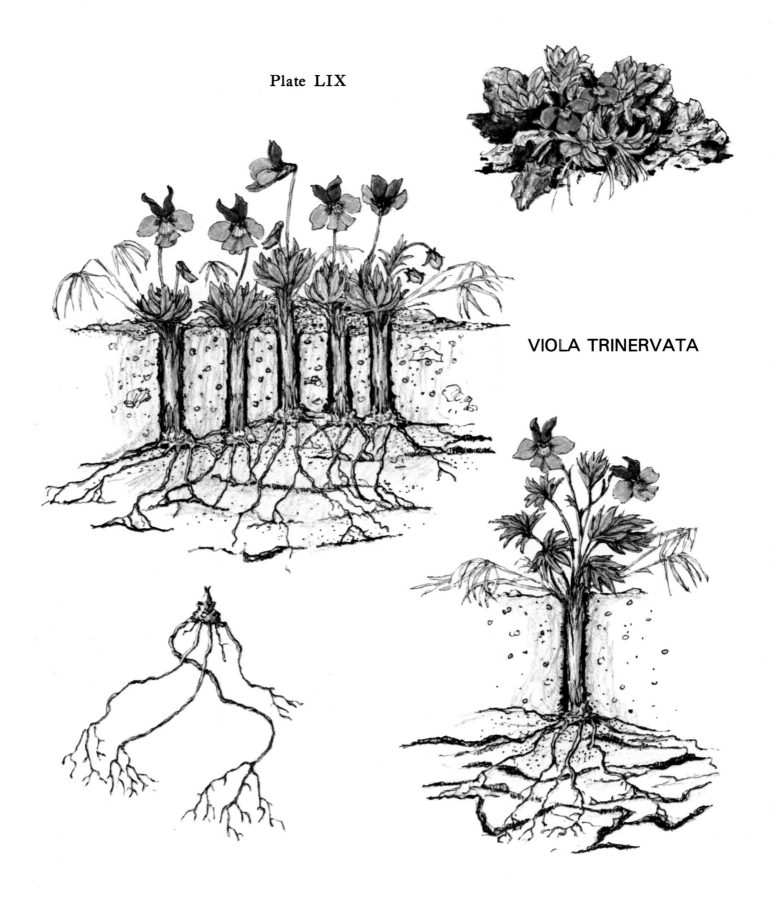

VIOLA ROSTRATA Pursh.

The Long-Spurred Violet

Plate XLVII

The Long-spurred Violet really lives up to its name. When in bloom the shape of the flower with its spur, perhaps a half-inch long, can hardly be confused with any other stemmed blue violet.

Viola rostrata has a wide range from Michigan south, in New England, and from the Appalachians to the mountains of Georgia. I introduced it into my woods (mixed deciduous) and it has felt much at home, spreading here and there but never a weed or pest. One seedling appeared in the crack of a huge boulder and that plant is by far the most prosperous. In fall it never disappears entirely, but keeps a central cluster of very green leaves, then spraying stems that may be six to eight inches long.

The basal leaves are always more rounded; the stem leaves get more and more pointed as they near the terminal. The stipules, long and narrow, draw to a fine point and have spiny hairs on the edges. I have drawn *V. rostrata* in various stages of its growth, for the early and late plants have a lot of purple in them, reminiscent of *V. labradorica* and *V. Walteri*.

The bearded flowers on long stems have a long season of bloom—from May to July. They vary in color from the rare white sent me from Connecticut, to the typical pale lavender with darker purple markings, to almost pink with a red-purple center. The spur may be curved or straight. The flowers held above the leaves never fail to delight you. The rootstock is woody.

As you see, the culture of *V. rostrata* is not complicated. Give it a well-drained, woodland soil in part shade, especially among rocks, and it will give you pleasure year after year. It is a fine plant for a shady rock-garden.

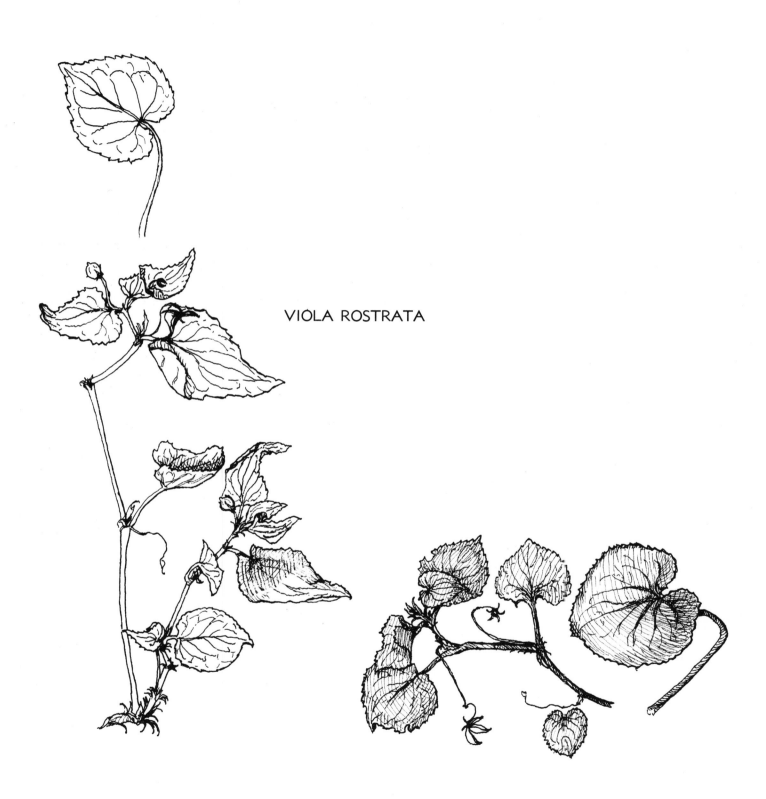

VIOLA ROSTRATA

VIOLA PALUSTRIS L.

The Marsh Violet

Plate XLVIII

Viola palustris is one of the circumpolar species found in cold bogs, along mountain streams, or other cold moist positions in Alaska, the northern Rockies and the White Mountains of New Hampshire. Helen White, who sent the white form from Alaska, said it came from a shrub-shaded, moist, gravelly bank with soil on the acid side. It is sometimes confused with the white-flowered *V. pallens* (*Viola Macloskeyi pallens*), as they both have rather rounded, light-green, smooth leaves. However, the early leaves of *V. palustris* are larger than those of *V. pallens* and they are more notice-ably scalloped than *V. Macloskeyi*. In addition, the typical flowers of *V. palustris* are pale lavender (like those sent from Montana—the lower left plant on Plate XLVIII), while those of *Macloskeyi* are always white. Another distinguishing point is that the petioles of *V. pallens* are almost invariably pubescent; those of *V. palustris* are smooth.

Given a half-shaded or open, moist position in well-drained, good soil, these violets respond rapidly to cultivation.

VIOLA EPIPSELA Ledeb.

Northern Marsh Violet

Plate XLIX

Although *V. palustris* and *V. epipsela* come from similar positions and have many points in common, they also have definite differences. Both have creeping rootstocks that produce runners, flowers pale violet or white and a short spur, but the shape of the flower differs and the spur of *V. epipsela* is much heavier than that of *V. palustris*. The leaves of *V. palustris* are thin, round, and pale green—a color that only the white form of *V. epipsela* (received from Alaska) shows. The typical leaves of *V. epipsela* are substantial and firm and come a bit more to a point than those of *V. palustris*. They have purplish petioles and peduncles, with some of this color in the leaves.

The lavender plants shown came from Aline Strutz of Anchorage, Alaska, where she says it grows in wet mossy thickets. These were received as one clump, but when I started to draw it, I found that it separated readily into three plants.

In a half-shaded, moist position it should be possible to cultivate *V. epipsela*. All the plants from marshes and wet places, with a few exceptions, require good drainage. If you go into swampy land you will note that most of the plants grow in humps of grasses, where they can reach water, but do not *stand in it*. There are a few additional cultural notes on the Alaskan species on the next Plate (*Selkirkii*).

115

VIOLA SELKIRKII Pursh.

Great Spurred Violet

Plate L

Viola Selkirkii is another circumpolar species. It is found from New England to the far west, including Alaska. Although old descriptions put it with the stemless group of violets, from the illustration you can see that it has a stem. It has stolons or runners and in good acid soil, such as hemlock woods or on decaying logs, it spreads into mats.

The leaves are symmetrical, slightly hairy on the upper surface, scalloped, heart-shaped, frequently overlapping at the base. The whole plant is lovely.

The color of the flower varies, depending on the amount of light and shade and the make-up of the soil. They are usually a light violet, veined darker, no beards, but white at the base of the petals. They start low and then gradually stretch out from one to four inches high. The spur is large and heavy as its common name indicates. They bloom toward the end of April. The upper picture on Plate L was from a photograph and the lower one was from a slide, both sent to me from Alaska, as was the plant with roots. The other plant came from Minnesota.

Aline Strutz wrote me of their Alaskan violets: "I'm afraid any directions I might give you would sound like your general directions for growing plants from seed—just put them in the ground and they grow! Actually it may not be as easy as that for folks living in warmer climates with hot summers and lots of dry weather, but for me it has been as simple as that. The beds that I use for rock-garden and wildflower plants are raised above the general level for good drainage, the soil contains some peat and sand. I have never fertilized any of my wildflowers, but I don't say that they couldn't occasionally benefit from it!"

VIOLA SELKIRKII

VIOLA FLETTII Piper

Olympic or Rock Violet

Plates LI, LII

Viola Flettii, native to the Olympic Mountains in Washington and pride of the state, is protected in the Olympic National Park. Since it is almost impossible to secure a plant, I have had to rely on a black and white photograph for the illustration on Plate LI. The photograph was taken by Carl S. English and published in the *Bulletin of the American Rock Garden Society.* English wrote that, "it grows in the high, windswept crags of the Olympics frequently in narrow, half-shaded crevices, and seems to prefer north or east exposure."

The shape of the leaves and their veining, and the shape of the flowers and their general appearance as *V. Flettii* grows among the rocks, were evident from the excellent photograph. For the color I depended on descriptions from Brainerd's *Violets of North America* and Abrams' *Flora of the Pacific*

States. The line drawing was adapted from one in Brainerd's book.

The flowers are a soft reddish-violet, veined darker with some yellow at the base and yellow beards on the laterals. The capsules are roundish and purple. The plant blooms at about 4500 feet from June to August.

Albert Sutton, who lives in Seattle, Washington, wrote me that he had collected *Viola Flettii* outside the park, but that it is difficult to keep because it is a favorite of slugs. He found it on a talus slope and it grew for a while in his garden. I sent him my drawing for criticism.

If one could get seeds and eventually plants, the only hope of success in cultivating it would seem to be screelike conditions in a very well-drained rock-garden.

VIOLA TRICOLOR L.

Johnny-Jump-Up

Plates LIII, LIV

While the Johnnies are not native-born, they have made themselves so at home in our gardens that we must include them in any discussion of our native violets. They may be tricolored, bicolored, or of a single tone, like 'The Black Imp.' They can be treated as annuals—the plants pulled up after they have finished flowering, and the many seeds shaken around in any spot where you want more the following year. In any case, they will no doubt volunteer in your garden and are easy to pull out if you don't want them right there. I never know what amusing combination of color is going to come up, so I rarely have the courage to throw any away. They are high in the affections of all true gardeners, adding piquancy to any planting.

The plants start to bloom while low and neat, but the stems gradually lengthen. When they begin to get weedy looking, it is good practice to give them a haircut so they will renew their bloom on a more compact plant.

The botanical details, if you need them to recognize these pets, are: leaves variously toothed on short petioles, petals longer than the sepals (which however are not noticeably long) and conspicuous comb-like stipules. They hybridize with other violets in their vicinity so that your collection may include large flowers on sturdy plants or real miniatures in both leaf and flower.

VIOLA ODORATA L.

The Sweet Violet

Plate LV

Viola odorata is a species that has come to us from Europe, where it has long been cultivated, and it has also been a florist's flower in this country. Like so many that have migrated to these shores it has made itself at home and has naturalized in many areas, in the course of time developing many colored forms. The plants illustrated all came from Pennsylvania.

Viola odorata has several easily recognizable features. It blooms ahead of most of the other violets; it has a sweet odor when in the sun or brought into a warm house; its dark-green glossy leaves are heart-shaped and regularly scalloped; it makes runners that root and form new plants.

While *Viola odorata* will bloom almost anywhere, it seems to do best in a soil with an acid reaction (as around azaleas and rhododendrons) that is rich in humus. It will grow in the sun, but half-shade is perhaps preferred. Frequent division after the blooming period seems to agree with the plant, the long rooting runners making this easy.

It has not spread fast here, but if you go out on a warm day in early spring, before other violets are in bloom, you suddenly get a whiff of its sweet odor. When you investigate you may find a few *V. odorata* where you remembered putting them, but you are just as likely to find that some have moved to a spot they prefer!

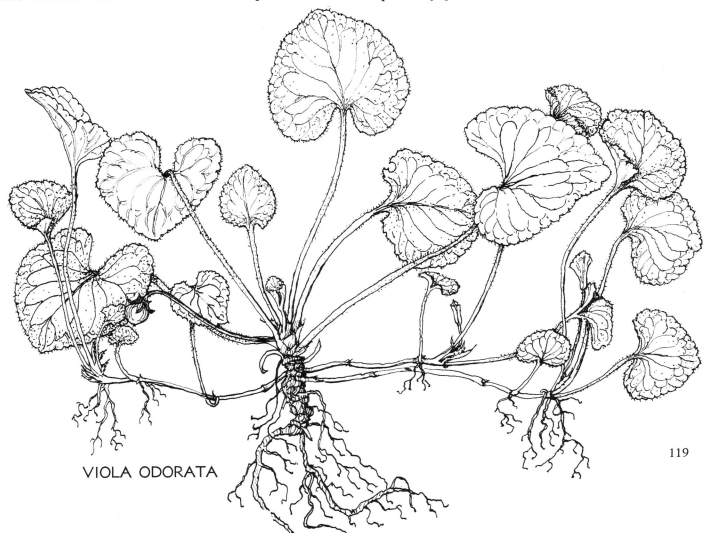

VIOLA ODORATA

119

VIOLA ODORATA L.

Western Sweet Violet

Plate LVI

In May 1967 I received a plant of *V. sempervirens* from the Siskiyou Nursery in Oregon. Embedded with the plant was a seedling with very woolly foliage, which was evidently a violet but certainly not *V. sempervirens.* I planted it separately and noticed that as it grew it produced runners that eventually rooted at their tips. It began to look more and more like *V. odorata,* though paler in tone of leaves and without the glossy upper surface, but much more pubescent. At last a few violets bloomed, the delicate little purple ones shown at the side of the plant, which were intensely fragrant. There could be no further doubt that I had received a western form of the sweet violets shown on Plate LV. These were all from Pennsylvania, though my own had originally come from somewhere in the midwest. By way of contrast I show a small plant of the eastern sweet violet on the plate with the western.

GROUP IV

STEMMED BLUE
CUT-LEAVED

Violas Beckwithii
trinervata
Hallii

VIOLA BECKWITHII Torr. & Gray

Beckwith's, Great Basin or Sagebrush Violet

Plate LVII

Viola Beckwithii is frequently confused with *Viola trinervata* (which was once considered a variety of it). This is not surprising if you look only at the flowers, as some forms are very close in shape and color, and both are slightly sweet-scented. Even the leaves, which are quite different in shape and consistency, come up folded in spring so that their form is not evident. Both species have leaves with the sage-green color common to many desert plants. But if you look at the drawings of single leaves in the illustrations, which I flattened somewhat to be able to draw their actual shapes, you will see how different they are.

The leaves of *V. trinervata,* besides being thicker in texture and broader in segments, have the prominent "three-nerved" veins of its name. The leaves of *Beckwithii* may be pubescent or glabrous and are cut into fine segments. They grow two to five inches high with a long stem buried deeply underground, attached to a short rootstock with strong spreading roots. This manner of growth seems to be typical of most of the western violets.

The flowers usually stand well above the leaves —the upper petals dark red-violet; the three lower, lilac with a yellow area at the base. The capsules are green. The plants bear no cleistogenes. They bloom from March to May or even later in stony, moist, good soil that later dries out. The aboveground part of the plant dies down after seeding. They are native to Oregon, Idaho, Nevada, Utah, and California at high elevations. The plants illustrated both come from Oregon. The separate flower shows a color form variant.

V. Beckwithii is one of the most difficult violets to cultivate. The only hope of doing so in the east would be to grow it in good rock-garden soil, in sun or light shade, where it would receive adequate moisture in spring but could be kept comparatively dry in summer.

VIOLA TRINERVATA Howell

The Sagebrush Violet or
Three-nerved Violet

Plates LVIII, LIX

The drawings on Plate LIX were made from slides, a photograph, and a live root sent me by Charles Thurman of Spokane, Washington. His comments follow:

"Viola trinervata blooms in March among rocks, for protection from the blazing sun, and soon disappears in the hot soil to be baked until the spring rains bring it up again.

"It grows with the crown of the plant one or two inches below the desert floor, either on or near fractured scab rock. It is accustomed to drying out after blooming but the roots fan out and penetrate the small fissures in the rock and so get a 'toe-hold' where some moisture persists.

"In spring the stems bore a hole through the heavy clay soil, pushing old dead leaves ahead of them, then emit their rather thick palmately cut leaves at the surface, the larger lobes being three-nerved, hence its name. There are usually two flowers or a flower and a bud on each slender stem. The stems gradually elongate, growing two to three inches high. The color varies depending on soil, sometimes lighter, sometimes darker but always two-toned. Under cultivation it must have perfect drainage as the soil would not dry out enough to cure the roots. A vertical position between rocks is indicated."

The drawings on Plate LVIII were made from a live plant from Virginia Winegar of Tygh Valley, Oregon. Mrs. Winegar wrote: "We live in a narrow valley that extends east and west. Each side of the ridge has its own flora. The violets grow on the north side above the belt of oaks and pines in the very hottest place, south to southwestern exposure. The soil is gravelly to bouldery. I removed a number of small rocks before I started to dig. These violets grow in widely separated locations instead of being scattered around the hill like most wildlings. As soon as hot weather comes they disappear. Here, east of the Cascades, we have from ten to fifteen inches of rain in a year, much different from the valleys of West Oregon. We are close to the mountains and as we climb the annual rainfall increases."

VIOLA HALLII Gray

Miniature Pansy or Hall's Violet

Plates LX, LXI

This precious violet, which blooms from April to May, comes from Washington to Oregon and California. It has much of the appeal and some of the coloring of the Johnny-Jump-Up. The upper petals, on both front and back, are dark velvety purple to almost black. The lower petals are cream or sometimes yellowish, with a dark yellow center and dark lines. The laterals have a yellow beard. The flowers hold themselves above the leaves.

The leaves are glabrous, sometimes tinted purple. They grow from two to six inches high, are a light green and are two to three times dissected into narrow lobes.

A soil that is not too rich will keep them low and compact—a feature that adds greatly to their charm. Like so many of these western violets that disappear as soon as they have seeded, there are no cleistogenes.

They grow on gravelly banks or in open woods, wet in spring (but may be dry at flowering time) and they are close relatives of *V. Beckwithii* and *V. Douglasii,* the latter a yellow, cut-leaved species. Plate LX is a plant that lived over the winter in my garden and bloomed in spring. On Plate LXI the large plant came from Oregon; the small one was adapted from a monotone photograph in Gabrielson's *Western American Alpines.*

Fragrant, like the other two in this group, *Hallii* has particular value for rock-gardens in well-drained soil and in part-shade (especially in the east) where it will be found to be less difficult than the other two species.

GROUP V

STEMLESS WHITE
UNCUT

Violas blanda
        incognita
        Macloskeyi
        Macloskeyi pallens (or pallens)
        renifolia
        lanceolata
        lanceolata vittata
        occidentalis
        primulifolia

Because the four following species, *Violas blanda, incognita, Macloskeyi,* and *pallens* have so many similarities, many people tend to confuse them—myself included. Rather than describe each separately, I compare them, hoping that when you refer to the Plates all will be crystal clear. The descriptions begin on page 145.

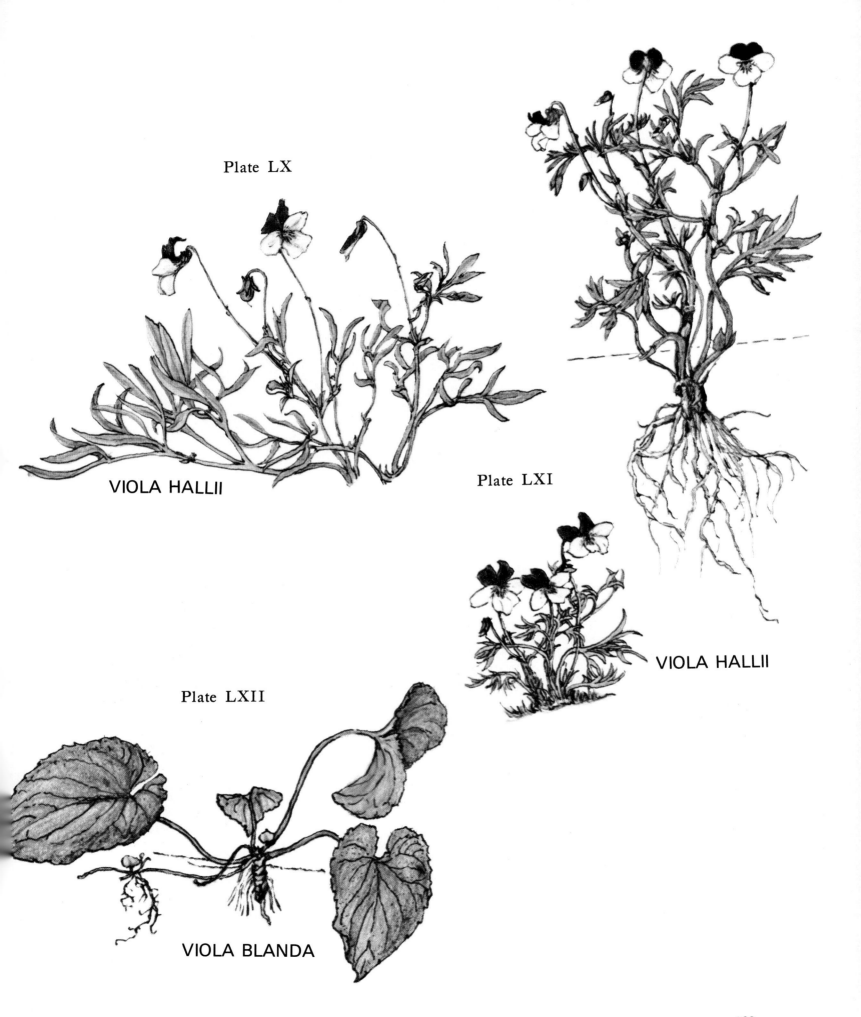

Plate LX

VIOLA HALLII

Plate LXI

VIOLA HALLII

Plate LXII

VIOLA BLANDA

129

Plate LXIII

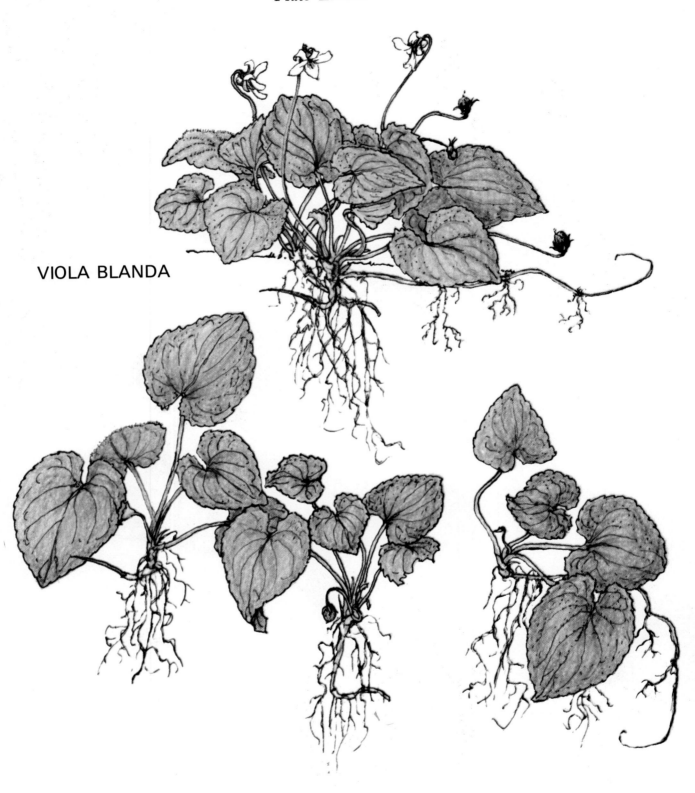

VIOLA BLANDA

Plate LXIV

VIOLA INCOGNITA

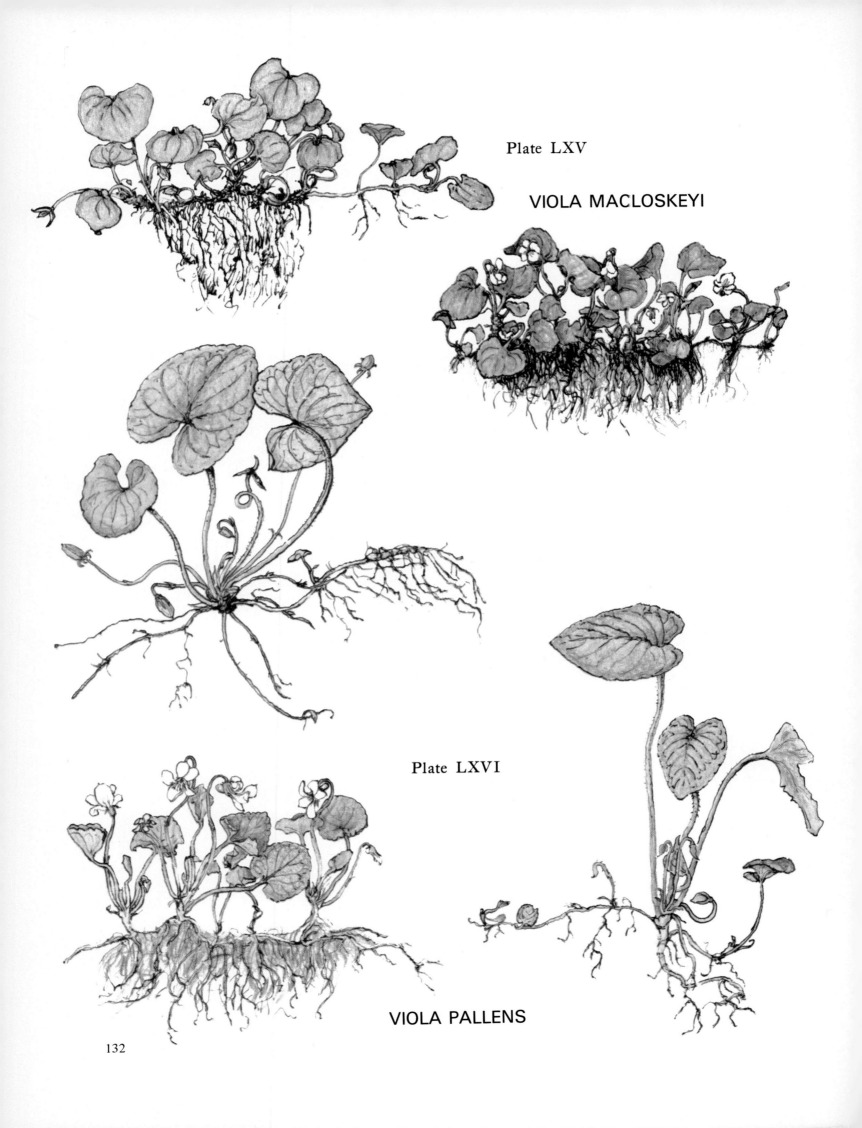

Plate LXV

VIOLA MACLOSKEYI

Plate LXVI

VIOLA PALLENS

132

Plate LXVII

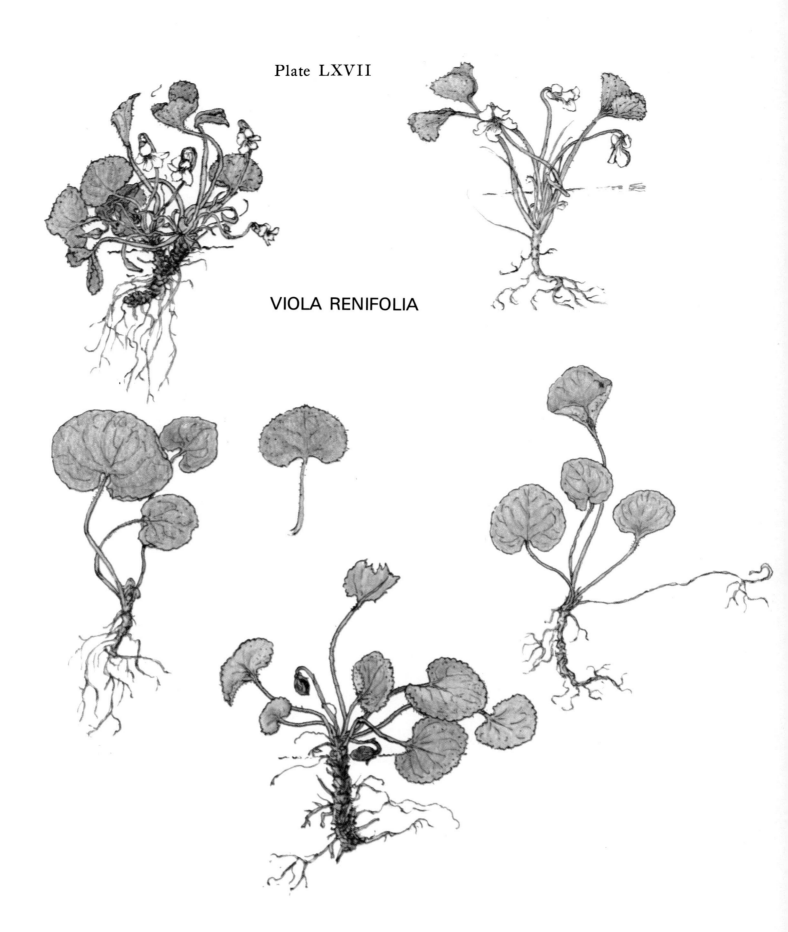

VIOLA RENIFOLIA

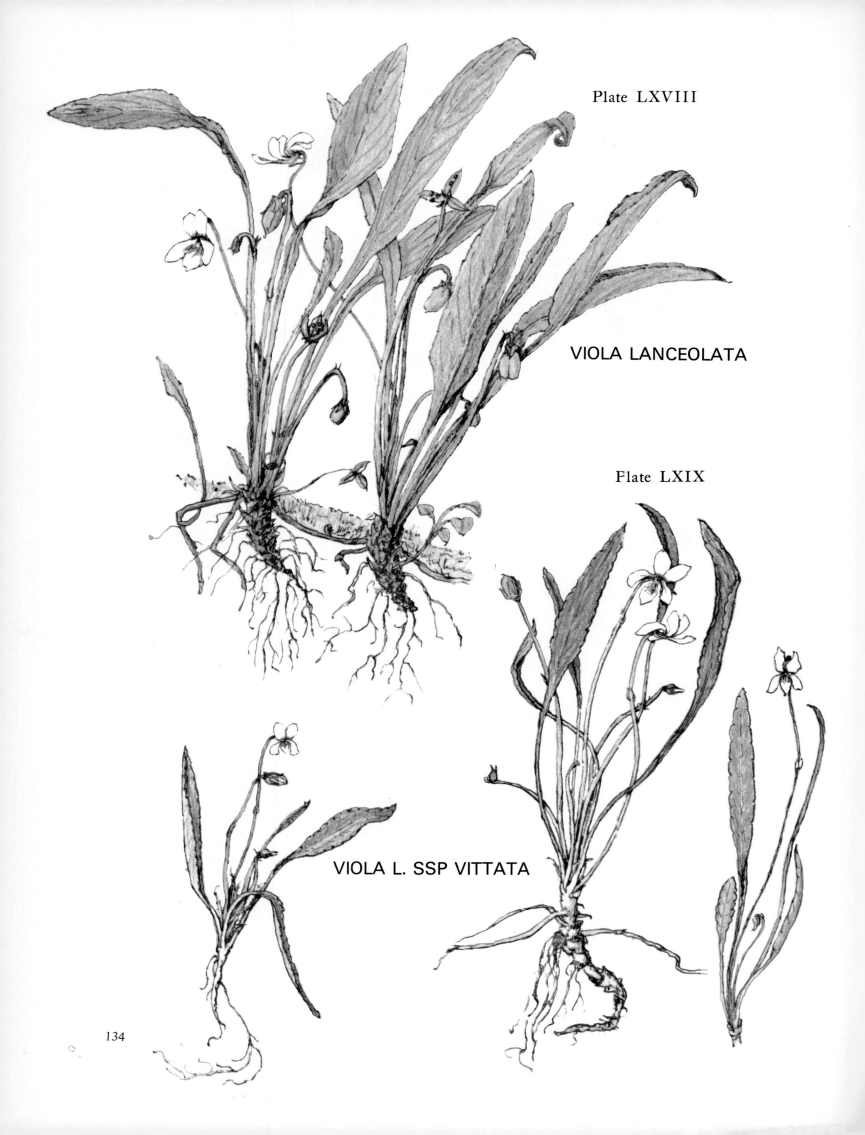

Plate LXVIII

VIOLA LANCEOLATA

Plate LXIX

VIOLA L. SSP VITTATA

134

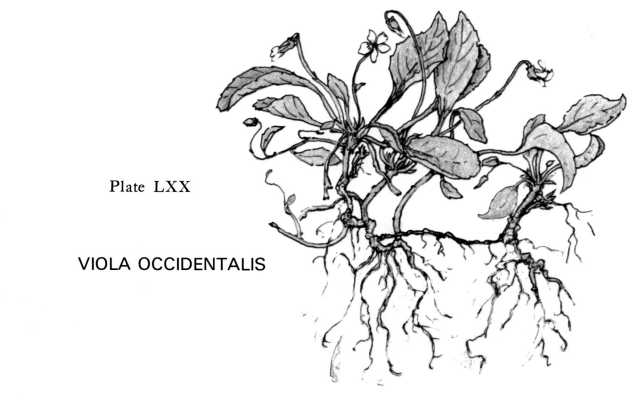

Plate LXX

VIOLA OCCIDENTALIS

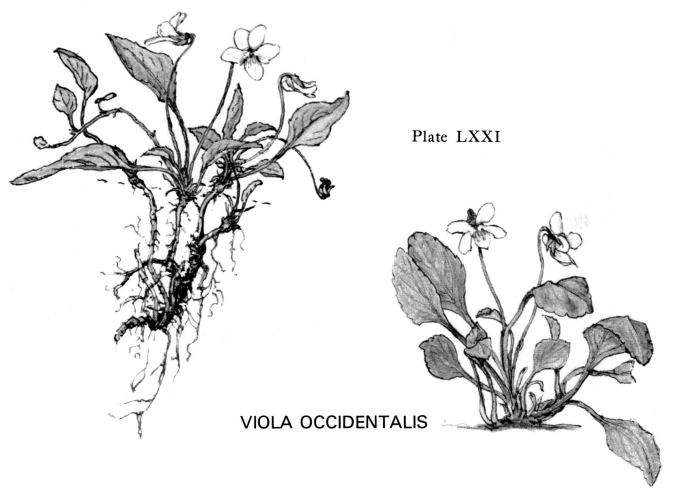

Plate LXXI

VIOLA OCCIDENTALIS

Plate LXXII

VIOLA PRIMULIFOLIA

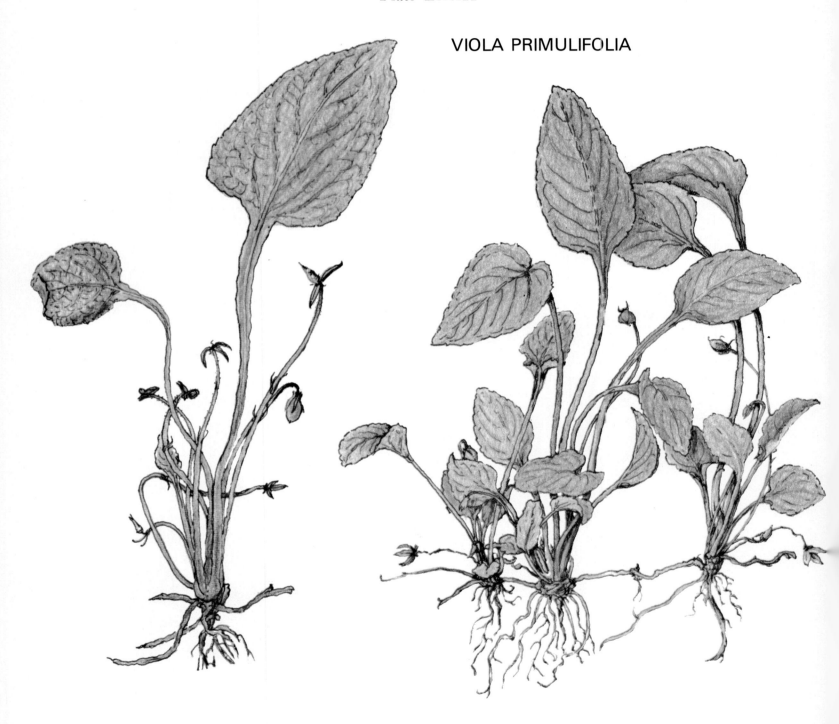

Plate LXXIII

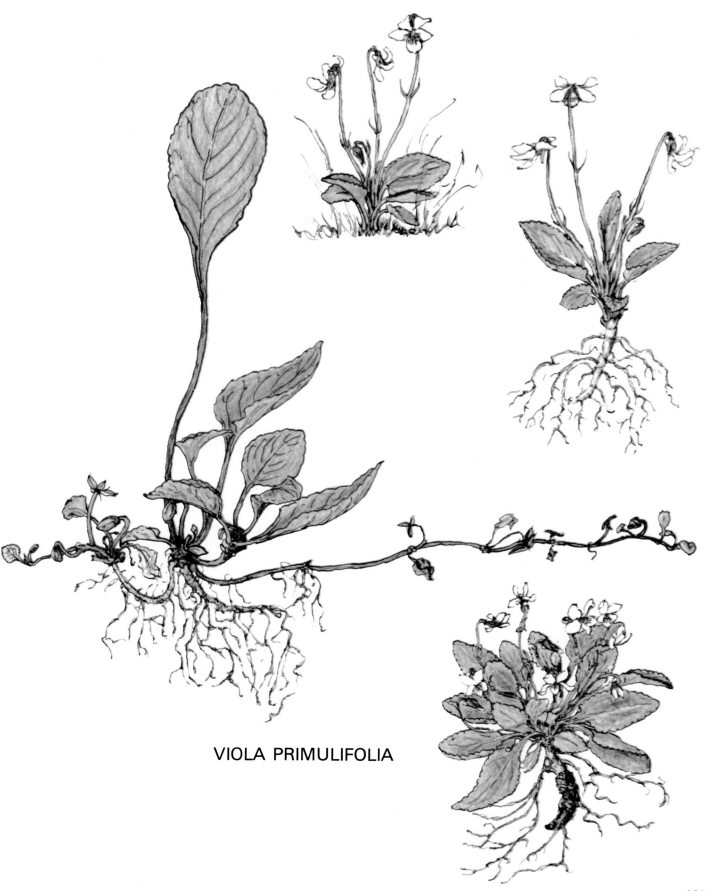

VIOLA PRIMULIFOLIA

Plate LXXIV

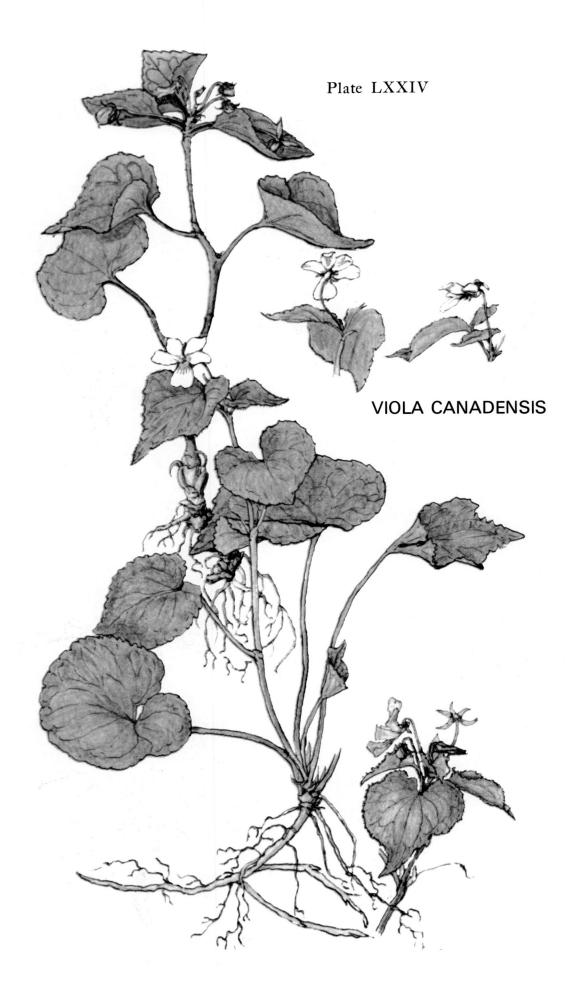

VIOLA CANADENSIS

Plate LXXV

VIOLA RUGULOSA

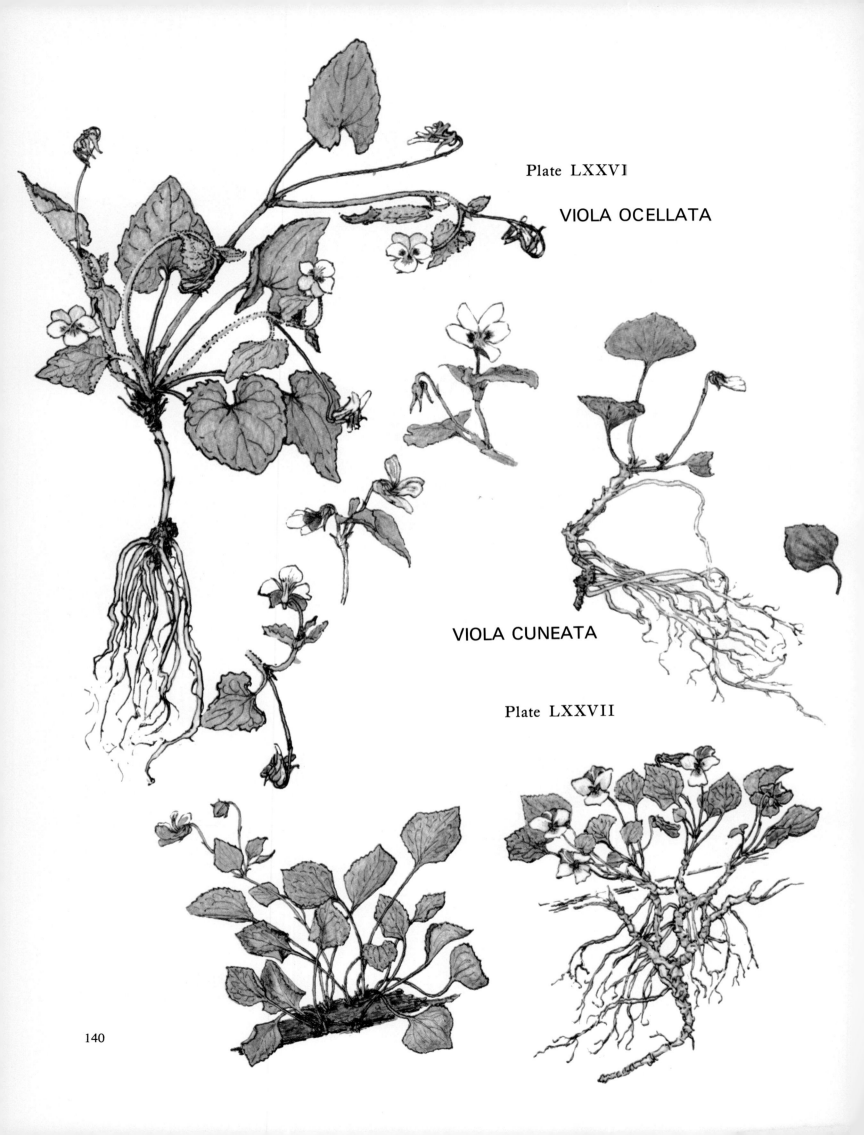

Plate LXXVI

VIOLA OCELLATA

VIOLA CUNEATA

Plate LXXVII

140

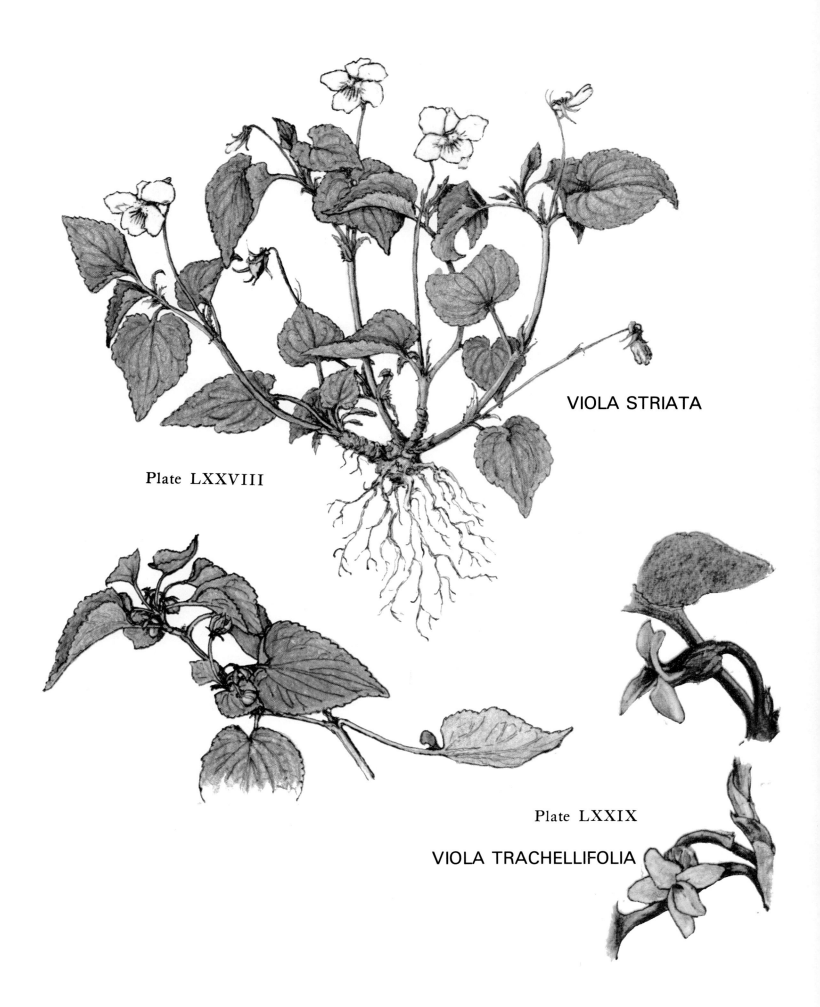

VIOLA STRIATA

Plate LXXVIII

Plate LXXIX

VIOLA TRACHELLIFOLIA

Plate LXXX

VIOLA TRACHELLIFOLIA

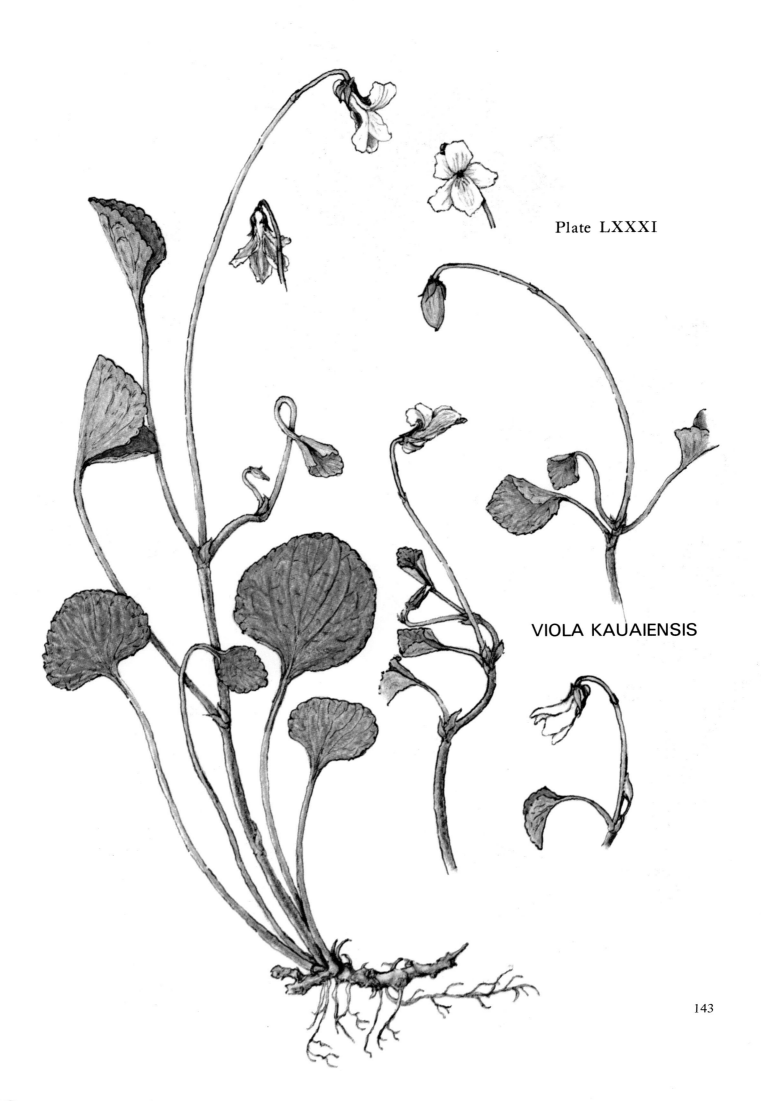

Plate LXXXI

VIOLA KAUAIENSIS

143

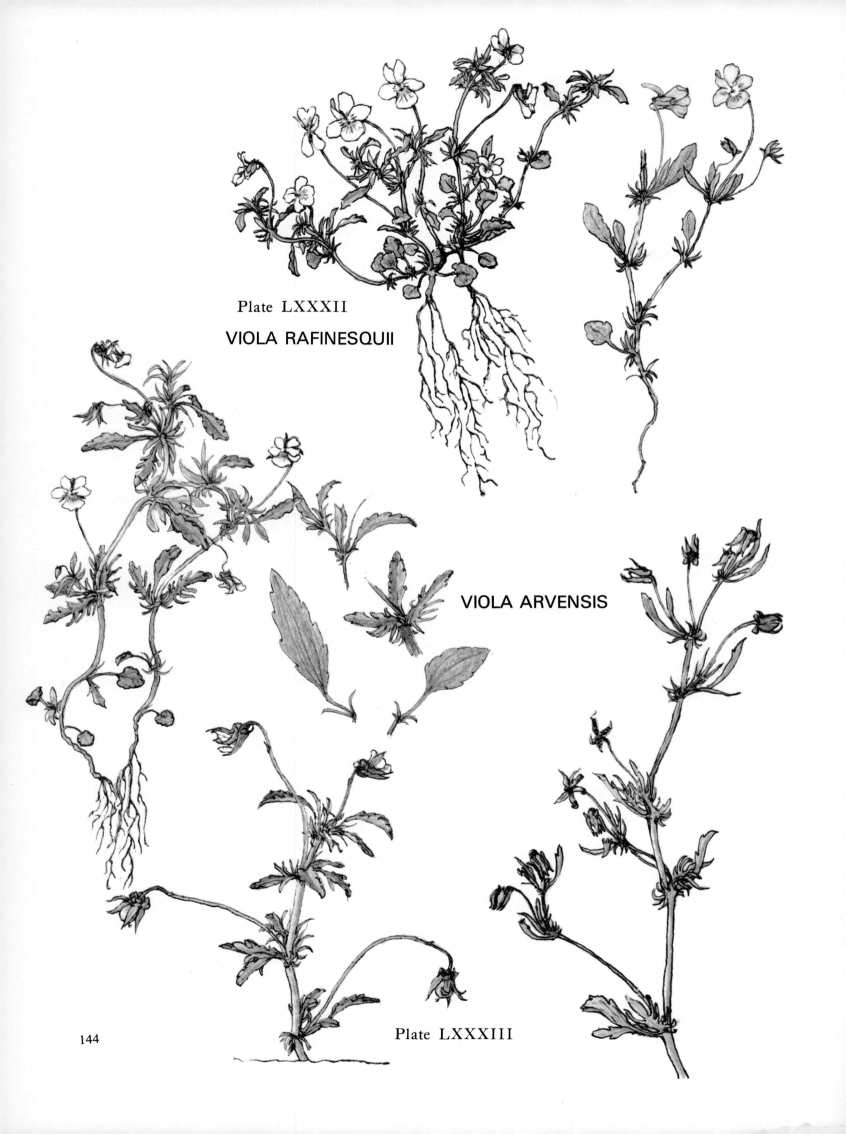

Plate LXXXII

VIOLA RAFINESQUII

VIOLA ARVENSIS

144

Plate LXXXIII

VIOLA BLANDA Willd.

Sweet White Violet

Plates LXII, LXIII

Violas blanda, incognita and *pallens* are all easterners, but *V. pallens* is so close to the western *V. Macloskeyi* that it is considered a subspecies of it and is now listed as *V. Macloskeyi,* ssp *pallens.*

Let us look at the easterners first. *Violas blanda* and *incognita* grow in damp woodland, while *V. pallens* comes from boggy or at least colder, moister positions than the other two.

The leaves of *V. blanda* are usually slightly hairy on the upper surface, with glabrous petioles.

The leaves of *V. pallens* are generally smooth or glabrous with pubescent petioles. On *V. blanda* the leaves are broad heart-shaped, with short lobes frequently overlapping at the base; the leaves of *V. incognita* are longer lobed and more open, while the leaves of *V. pallens* are usually oval in shape and very regularly patterned. They may all have some red on the leaves and petioles, but *V. blanda* is more conspicuously red, especially in moist positions and in its autumn color.

VIOLA INCOGNITA Brainerd

Woodland White Violet or Unrecognized Violet

Plate LXIV

The flowers of *V. blanda* have narrow, beardless petals that tend to reflex. *V. pallens* is also beardless, while *V. incognita* has a heavy beard. The cleistogenes of *V. blanda* and *V. incognita* are purplish and prostrate, while in *V. pallens* they are upright, green, and oblong in outline. *V. blanda* has an elusive fragrance as is sometimes noticeable in the other white violets too.

Viola blanda is a low, broad plant that is two to three inches high. It does not change much over the season except to get rosy autumn coloring. *V. incognita* is very flat, as shown on Plate LXIV, lying close on a mat of pine needles. *V. pallens* is a smaller plant than either of the others at flowering time, but gets taller later. They all have runners by which they spread.

Viola blanda is largely Appalachian in distribution but can be found as far south as Tennessee, Georgia, and southern Indiana. Those shown came from Vermont. Only in the south is it found at high altitudes. *Viola incognita,* while sometimes found near *V. blanda* in mixed forests that include hemlocks and pines, is also found as far west as the Great Lakes region. The one illustrated came from New York. *V. incognita* usually has greener stalks than the other two. *V. pallens* may be found in open bogs or springy land and also near the tops of mountains in Vermont and Massachusetts, in both sun and shade.

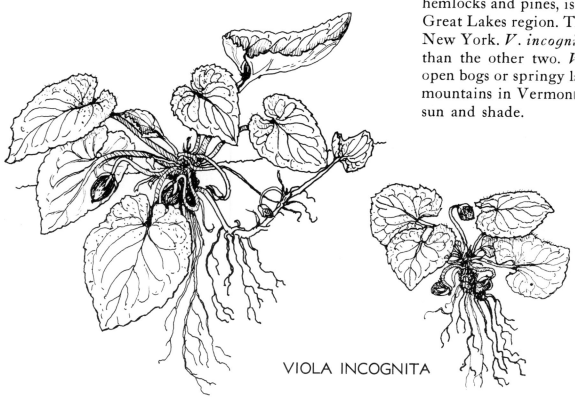

VIOLA INCOGNITA

VIOLA MACLOSKEYI Lloyd

Macloskey's Violet

VIOLA PALLENS Brainerd

VIOLA MACLOSKEYI, ssp. PALLENS Baker

Smooth White Violet

Plates LXV, LXVI

The western *Viola Macloskeyi* can be found all along the west coast from Washington to southern California. Those shown on Plate LXV came from Oregon. The plants are low and matted, with thin, small leaves, suborbicular to broadly ovate, shallow-cordate at the base. This violet differs from its subspecies *V. pallens* in the outline of the leaves, which in *V. Macloskeyi* show only very small crenations (sometimes none) and have a sinuous outline. *V. pallens* has definite scalloping and its leaves come more to a point.

V. Macloskeyi is found in bogs and other moist positions.

A word of caution about pubescence in all violets. *It varies considerably* and cannot always be taken as a distinguishing mark, though Russell tells us that some forms of hairiness (as hairs on the petioles of *V. pallens*) seem to be hereditary.

VIOLA RENIFOLIA Gray

Northern White Violet

Plate LXVII

Viola renifolia is easily distinguished from the other white violets by its reniform or kidney-shaped leaves, beardless white flowers with dark lines and short spur, prostrate cleistogenes and lack of stolons. It may vary from smooth to hairy on the lower surface of the leaves and tops of petioles, to pubescent on both surfaces. Its slender rootstock becomes stout and scaly with age. The Alaskan form (those in flower, from separate stations) is a more compact plant than that received from New York State (opposite page). Christine Heller, in *Wild Flowers of Alaska,* writes that "it is a small, shy violet, easily overlooked."

Although Mrs. Heller lists it as from a roadside near Anchorage, it is usually found in deeply shaded evergreen forests, along cold ravines, or even in swampy land. It has a wide range over the eastern and north central states, and sometimes is found in the Rockies, in Colorado, and in northern Washington. Its small, white flowers are slightly fragrant.

In the west it is distinguished from *V. Macloskeyi* which has runners and grows in bogs. In the east it may be found associated with *Violas blanda* and *incognita,* but again the lack of runners and the shape of the leaves separates it.

Given good woodland conditions in an acid soil environment it should prove easy to grow. Judging by the various types of places in which it is found, it seems to be a most adaptable species.

VIOLA RENIFOLIA

VIOLA LANCEOLATA L.

The Lance-leaved Violet

VIOLA LANCEOLATA ssp. VITTATA Greene

(In New Jersey called The Pine Barrens Violet)

Plates LXVIII, LXIX

Viola lanceolata is found in sandy, moist, open situations, frequently along streams or ponds. It is prevalent along the northeastern coast and as far west as Minnesota. The illustration is of a Pennsylvania plant. Its subspecies *V. vittata* is more likely to be found from Pennsylvania south and along the Gulf Coast. Those shown came from Florida, the New Jersey Pine Barrens and Texas.

Both can be quite small at flowering time, growing taller with age. The narrow glabrous leaves taper at both ends, the lower end extending into margined petioles. They are slightly toothed in *V. lanceolata* and more regularly scalloped in *V. vittata*. The plants bear long stolons, frequently red, that root freely and bear new plants at their tips the following year.

Their white flowers have purple lines, are beardless, and are even with or slightly exceeding the leaves in height. They bear many cleistogenes. In the east the plant hybridizes freely with *V. primulifolia* and *V. pallens*.

Viola occidentalis from Washington, Oregon, and California is considered by some botanists to be another subspecies of *V. lanceolata,* which has become established in Washington cranberry bogs and other wet, marshy land. See Plates LXX and LXXI.

Both *V. lanceolata* and *V. vittata* can be cultivated in open, sandy, moist areas.

150

VIOLA OCCIDENTALIS Gray

VIOLA LANCEOLATA, ssp. OCCIDENTALIS (Gray) Russell

Western Water Violet

Plates LXX, LXXI

This enticing little plant seems to be a separate species from the attractive but different *V. lanceolata*. Both species are, of course, white-flowered, have leaves tapering at both ends, and make runners—but there the likeness seems to stop. It is true that in a photograph in Gabrielson's *Western American Alpines* the leaves look taller and broader, as they do in an illustration in Brainerd's *Violets of North America,* but in both cases they look more like the leaves of *V. primulifolia* than of *V. lanceolata.* My drawings were made from live plants sent me by the Siskiyou Nursery in Oregon. The small-flowered plant probably came into bloom in transit; the larger one was sent in bloom later in the season. Its long season of bloom is one of its attractions.

Viola occidentalis grows in open, sunny bogs with *good drainage,* along the Pacific Coast in Oregon and California. It is three to six inches high, has glabrous leaves (slightly crenate), a vertical branching rootstock with fibrous roots, and thin fibrous runners that root and produce new growth. The leaves and flowers grow vertically, the latter even with or slightly overtopping the leaves. There are no cleistogenes. The leaves are spoon-shaped to elliptic, the peduncles and petioles slightly reddish.

The pure-white flowers have dark-purple lines and are bearded. The spurs are short.

Boyd Kline says these violets have to be babied in cultivation, unless you can give them a position close to their natural habitat.

151

VIOLA PRIMULIFOLIA L.

Primrose-leaved Violet

Plates LXXII, LXXIII

Viola primulifolia, found along the eastern and Gulf coasts and also further inland, is a clean, gay-looking plant. It is so variable that I show several forms. Those on Plate LXXII came from North Carolina and Pennsylvania; those on Plate LXXIII from South Carolina and New York, while the small plant at the bottom is probably a hybrid. Like *V. lanceolata* it is a plant of moist, open places and violets of these species frequently grow near each other.

The leaves, glabrous in the north, may be pubescent farther south. They are likely to be red near the base of the petioles, then turn green as they wing out and blend into the blades of the leaves, which frequently show some red on back and veins.

The long-blooming flowers are brightened at the center with green pistil and orange stamens, while the pedicels are pinkish. The cleistogenes grow erect with green capsules. The plants spread by pink, leafy stolons rooting at the nodes.

Give them a moist, open, well-drained position.

GROUP VI

STEMMED WHITE
UNCUT

Violas canadensis
       canadensis variety rugulosa
       ocellata
       cuneata
       striata
       trachellifolia
       kauaiensis
       Rafinesquii
       arvensis

VIOLA CANADENSIS L.

VIOLA RUGULOSA Greene

Canadian Violet and var. Rugulosa

Plates LXXIV, LXXV

Speaking of *Viola canadensis* from both the east and the far west, and *V. rugulosa* from the midwest (*V. canadensis* var. *rugulosa*), Dr. Russell says, "In my opinion, *Viola rugulosa* is a violet of the northern plains and Rockies. There are some in Wisconsin, but it gets no further east." *V. rugulosa* is said to produce long stolons and *V. canadensis* is said not to. This is true *most* of the time *but not always*. It can be seen, on Plate LXXIV, that of the two *Violas canadensis* shown (from Vermont and Pennsylvania), one has an ordinary heavy rootstock, the other stolons.

In *rugulosa* from Colorado, Plate LXXV, the purple color on the back of the petals showed through the thin-textured flowers, giving them a lavender tinge. On the white firmer petaled *V. canadensis* on the same plate, the tinge on the back of the petals did not show through. In October the color of *V. canadensis* deepened, showing red on the buds and pinkish flowers.

I received some very coarse plants from Vermont labeled *V. rugulosa,* which turned out to be *canadensis.* I also received coarse plants from Montana labeled *V. rugulosa.* These had *no stolons.*

All this, I think, only emphasizes how similar the two plants are, and we gardeners can leave the verbal skirmishes on the matter to the botanists.

Both plants are of comparatively easy culture in many parts of the country. They are both woodland species from open, well-drained positions in half-shade. Planted in my acid-soil corner, *V. canadensis* continued to bloom into late fall.

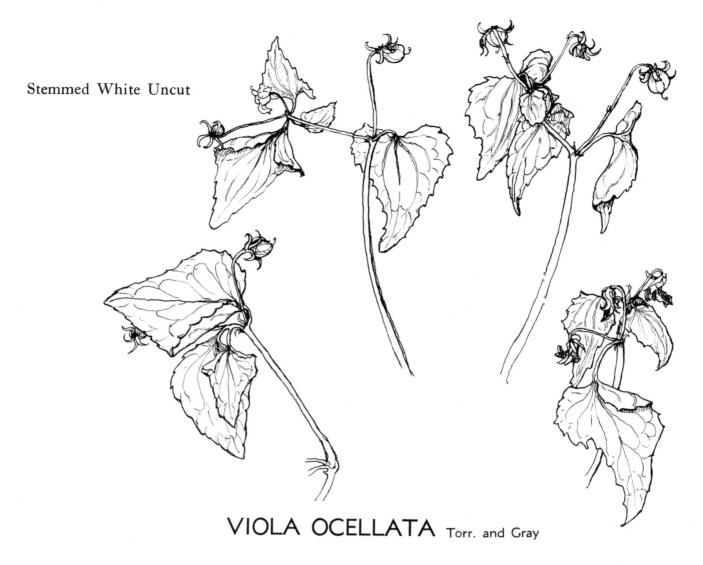

VIOLA OCELLATA Torr. and Gray

Two-eyed Violet or Pinto Pansy

Plate LXXVI

This appealing violet comes from wooded slopes in the loose duff along mountain trails in mixed coniferous forests. Its upper petals are deep reddish-purple on the back, showing through with a lavender tinge on the front. The side petals are marked with short purple lines that blur into a spot or "eye," while the lower petal is purple-striped. There is yellow in the center of the flower and sometimes the three lower petals are tinted yellow. They have a long flowering season. Dorothy Young of Gualala, California, sent me the plant and says that in their section it blooms all summer.

The flowers grow from the axils of the leaves on fairly long pedicels, even with or slightly lower than the leaves.

The long, slender rootstock, scaly at the joints, emits many strong roots. The leaves are usually heart-shaped though occasionally cuneate at the base; the basal leaves, as so often is the case, are larger than the stem-leaves.

Although its manner of growth is somewhat like that of *V. canadensis,* there are a number of obvious differences: pubescence appears on *V. ocellata,* but not on *V. canadensis* (though *V. rugulosa* has some) ; the shape and coloring of flowers are not the same, and the root growth differs.

On a well-drained, wooded slope or other half-shaded position in acid-soil conditions, one should be able to cultivate this violet on the home grounds.

VIOLA CUNEATA Watson

The Wedge-leaved Violet

Plate LXXVII

It is a comfort when one violet has some definite difference that separates it from others. The western, rather rare, *Viola cuneata* can be recognized by its cuneate (wedge-shaped) leaves, acute at the apex and attenuate at the base, crenate on the edges. The leaves may be purple on the back and veined purple. As usual, the basal leaves are larger than the stem-leaves, on longer petioles and occasionally heart-shaped at the base.

The adorable little flowers grow from the axils of the upper leaves, even with or surpassing them. On the typical plant the petals are all purple on the back. In front, the upper pair of petals is purple with a white edge; the three lower petals are white or have a tinge of lavender showing through from the back. There are purple spots at the center of the flowers, with a yellow base and purple lines on the lower petal. The capsules are said to be purple. Ira N. Gabrielson writes of *V. cuneata* as a "fat-faced white flower with deep purple spots on each cheek, making an amusing effect." I show a young plant from Oregon of the rare white form that is white on both front and back.

Viola cuneata is found in Oregon and California. Boyd Kline wrote me from Oregon, "*Viola cuneata* grows and blooms in very moist conditions, usually on wet hillsides, but the clay soil dries quickly in summer, becoming caked around the roots. It grows in full, hot sun, occasionally under the shade of oaks." A description from California says that it grows in forests of fir, cedar, dogwoods, azaleas, and rhododendrons, which association would indicate a soil with an acid reaction.

Under cultivation in the eastern states it would probably do best in a well-drained rock-garden in part shade where it received ample water in early spring, or in pine or hardwood forests where the trees and undergrowth would drain off much of the water in summer. Good drainage, in my experience with these desert and mountain plants, is of the first importance.

Other violets found in similar conditions in California are: *Violas lobata, Hallii, adunca, occidentalis, palustris, sempervirens* and *glabella*.

VIOLA STRIATA Ait.

The Creamy Violet

Plate LXXVIII

Viola striata is an eastern species found from New York to Georgia and to Missouri. The purple lines (or striae) are really no more noticeable on this violet than on many others that also have them. The flowers grow on long pedicels from the axils of the leaves, and the backs of the petals are also white, not tinted lavender as in *canadensis*. The lateral petals are bearded.

Viola striata is recognized most readily by its large, fringed stipules and narrow, curving sepals. However, the appearance of the plant in spring and on into summer, with its many cream-white flowers, soon identifies it—even for a casual observer. The only time of year when it might confuse one is in very early spring, for the plants then make a close clump of dark-green leaves and start to bloom while quite small. One may question whether this neat little plant can be the same species that in summer reaches 18 to 24 inches in height, and after its long season of bloom, has such an abundance of seed-heads. The long branches spread around and in shade will make a ground-cover. It is more restrained in full sun.

The leaves do not vary as much as most violets. They are evenly toothed, and have shallow rounded lobes at the base and an acute point at the tip.

Viola striata's long season of bloom makes it a good plant to edge a driveway, where it will make a fine white-flowered border, then carry its leaves almost through the winter. Periodic trimming will keep it compact. It can drape a wall with white flowers if you want just one plant there. The only difficulty in cultivating it is to keep it from spreading where you don't want it!

It is close botanically to the blue-stemmed violets and will hybridize with them—which it does not do with the other stemmed white violets.

VIOLA TRACHELLIFOLIA Ging.

Woody Hawaiian Violet

Plates LXXIX, LXXX

Viola trachellifolia from Hawaii surprised me by being a woody plant that grows from one to six feet high! It was sent by the State Forester (at that time) M. F. Landgraf. He sent me woody cuttings, some live flowers in polyethylene bags, a pamphlet about their violets, and some good slides of plants and flowers. With this fine material I was able to prepare the plate.

Mr. Landgraf sent me not only parts of the plant from Oahu, which are shown in the drawings, but others from some of the other Hawaiian islands. Although they differ somewhat in appearance— some have larger leaves, some look more like lilac leaves, some have more or less pink in the flowers— they were all called *V. trachellifolia*.

In addition there are several other woody species and one deciduous one, *V. kauaiensis* (see Plate LXXXI) with glabrous leaves and stemmed, fra-grant flowers. *Viola odorata* has become natural-ized in some places.

For those interested in growing the various species, either in a greenhouse in the north or out-doors in the south, I append a list of the other woody violets. They all can probably be increased by layerings or by cuttings started in sand. A well-drained soil rich in humus seems to fulfill their needs.

The flowers shown on this page were probably more pink than yellow. The slide had been taken in full golden sunlight.

Other Woody Hawaiian Violets

Viola mauiensis ...... from Maui, Hawaii
Viola wailenalenae ... from Kauai
Viola Helenae .... from Kauai, Lanai
Viola oahuensis ...... from Koolau, Range of Oahu
Viola Chamissoniana . from Waianae Range, Oahu
Viola robusta .... from Molokai

VIOLA KAUAIENSIS Degener & Greenwell

Hawaiian Deciduous Violet

Plate LXXXI

Although *Viola odorata* has naturalized in Hawaii, *Viola kauaiensis* is the only native deciduous violet found there. It grows on Kauai and Oahu, and is said to be fragrant, though this was not noticeable when it was received in bloom by airmail in December 1966. Probably, like so many sweet-smelling violets, it needs sunshine and warmth to release its odor, or else it may be nocturnally fragrant, as many white flowers are, including another Hawaiian, *Viola chamissoniana.*

M. F. Landgraf, then State Forester, wrote me that *V. kauaiensis* was collected on December 15 from the bog area at the head of the Wahiawa Stream on the island of Kauai. It came, like most of my collection, in a tightly closed polyethylene bag free of soil, and still looked fresh when I opened it on December 22.

The face of the flower is cream white with purple guidelines and a somewhat ridged surface. The backs of the petals are marked with purple lines that blur together in places. There was one spray of an all-white form that was a much cleaner creamy white. The main stem and lower part of the petioles are tinged purple. The leaves are glossy, smooth, firm, rich green, somewhat lighter on the reverse, and regularly scalloped. They taper into the petioles at the bottom. The fruit is a green pod.

As it is deciduous it should "do"—at least in the warmer parts of the mainland.

Plate LXXXIV

VIOLA ROTUNDIFOLIA

Plate LXXXV

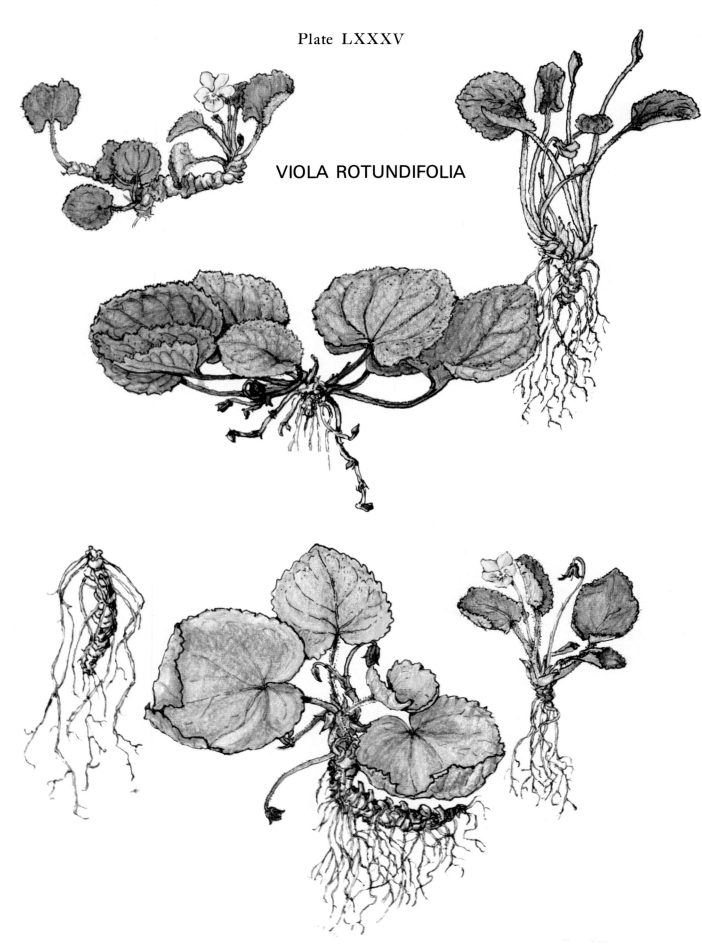

VIOLA ROTUNDIFOLIA

Plate LXXXVI

VIOLA BAKERI

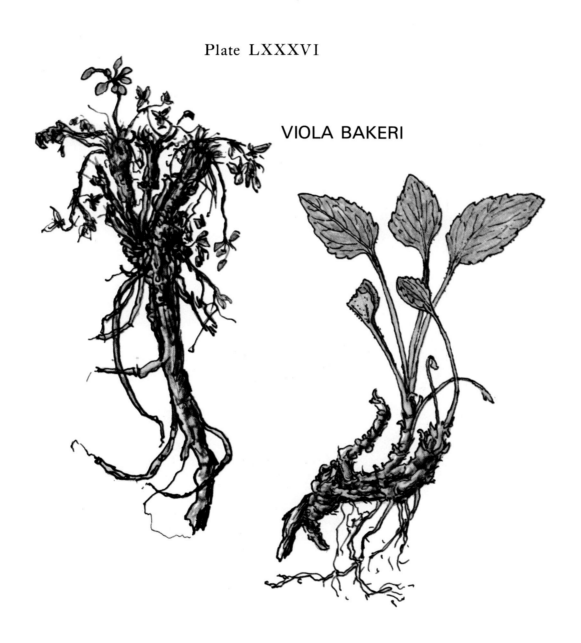

Plate LXXXVII

VIOLA NUTTALLII
VIOLA VALLICOLA

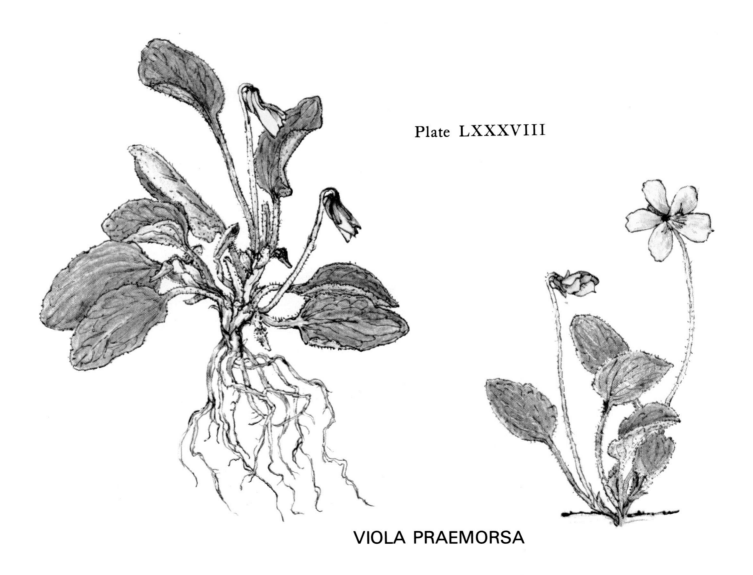

Plate LXXXVIII

VIOLA PRAEMORSA

Plate LXXXIX

VIOLA PRAEMORSA

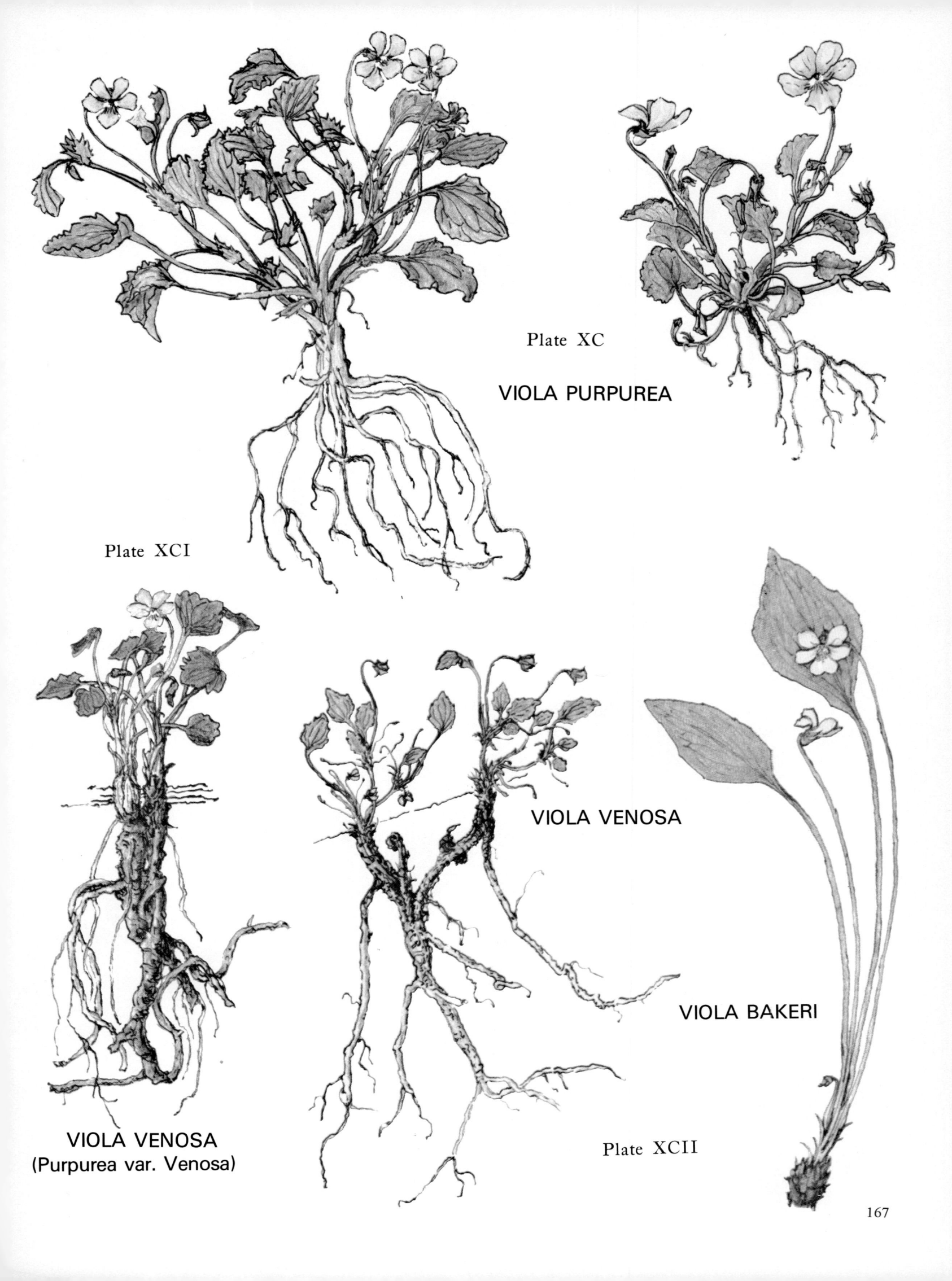

Plate XC

VIOLA PURPUREA

Plate XCI

VIOLA VENOSA

VIOLA BAKERI

VIOLA VENOSA
(Purpurea var. Venosa)

Plate XCII

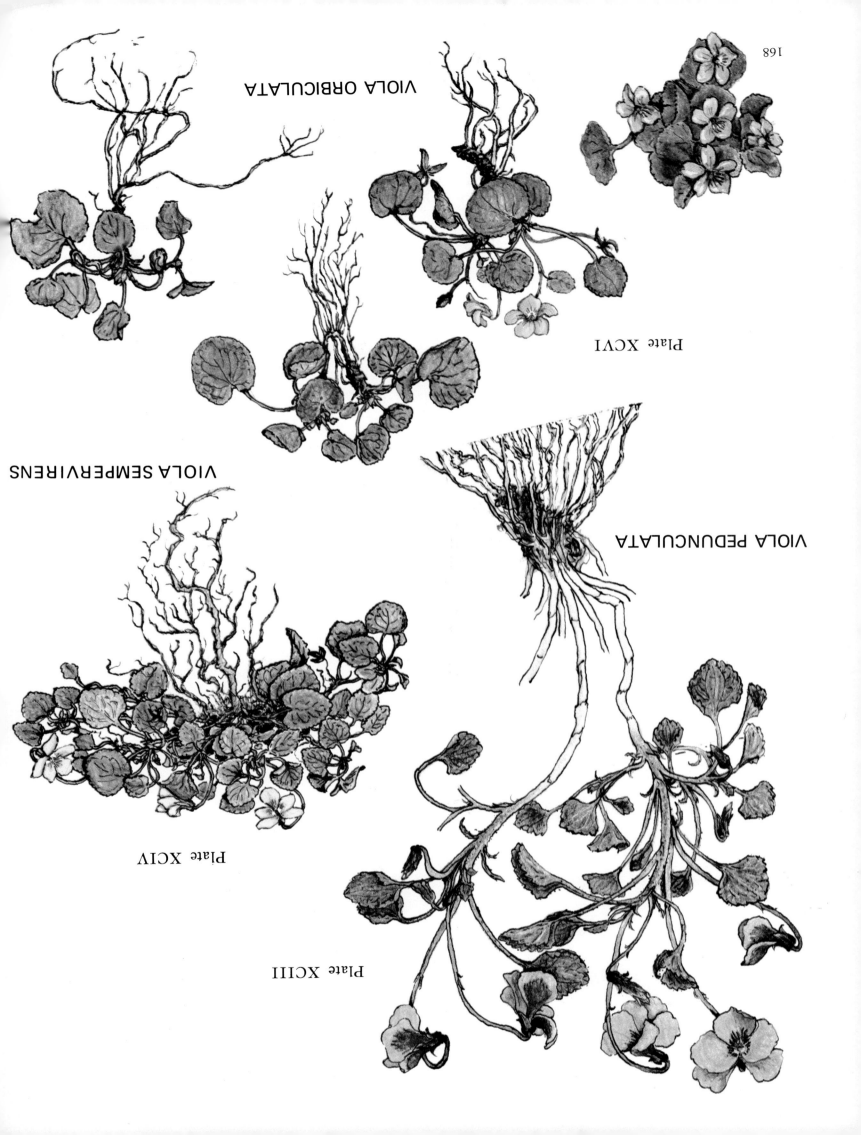

VIOLA ORBICULATA

168

Plate XCVI

VIOLA SEMPERVIRENS

VIOLA PEDUNCULATA

Plate XCIV

Plate XCIII

Plate XCV

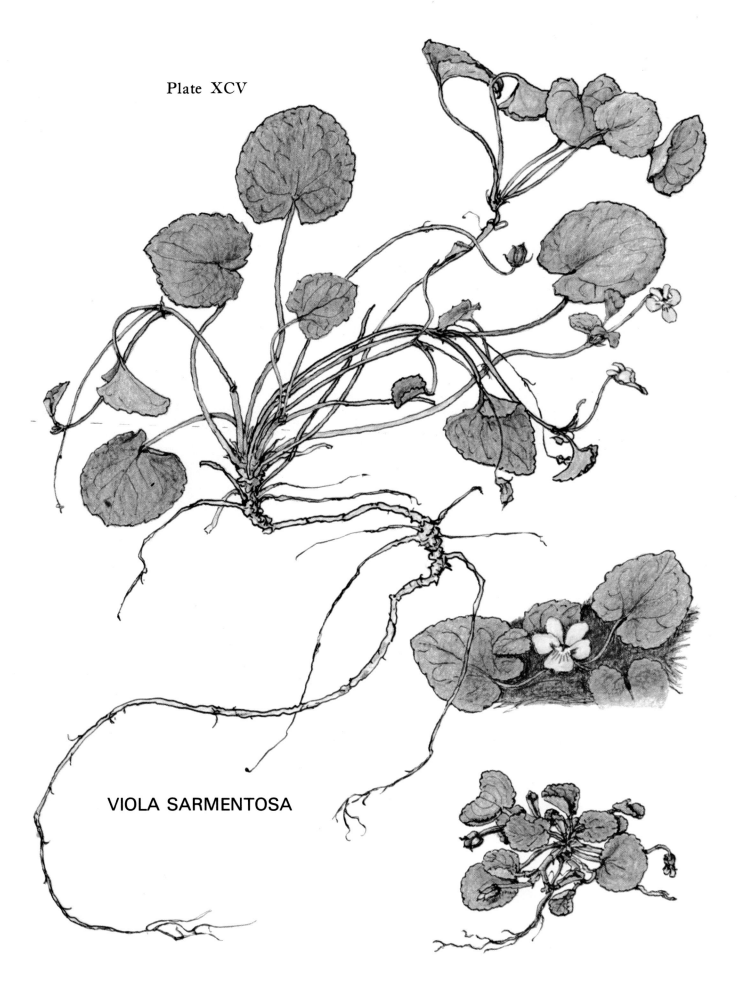

VIOLA SARMENTOSA

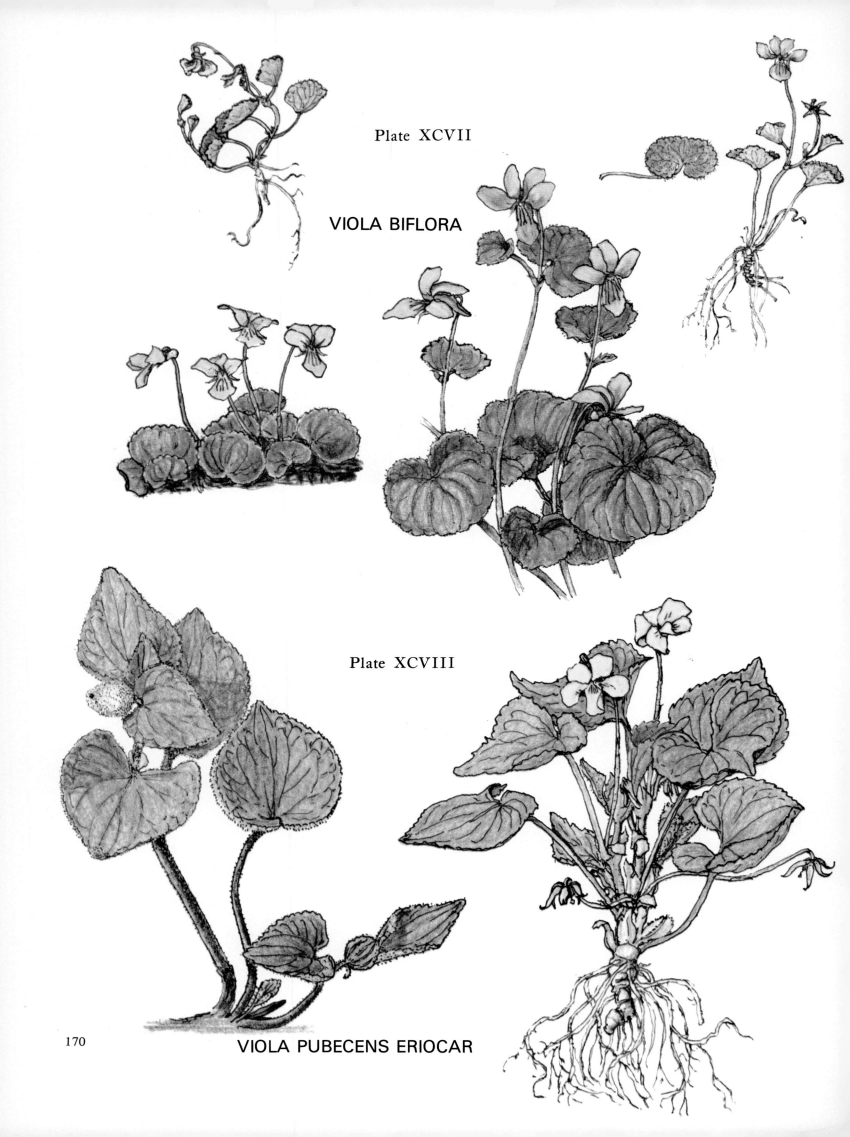

Plate XCVII

VIOLA BIFLORA

Plate XCVIII

170 VIOLA PUBECENS ERIOCAR

Plate XCIX

VIOLA PUBESCENS

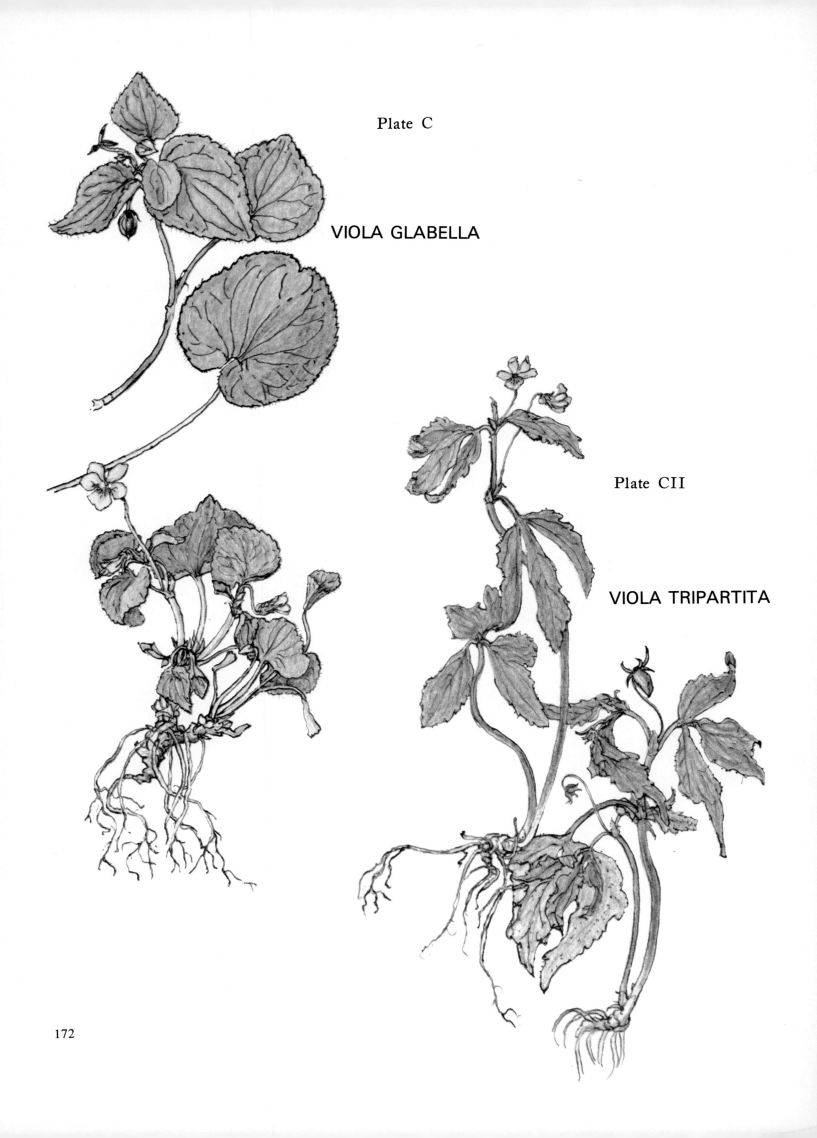

Plate C

VIOLA GLABELLA

Plate CII

VIOLA TRIPARTITA

Plate CI

VIOLA GLABELLA

173

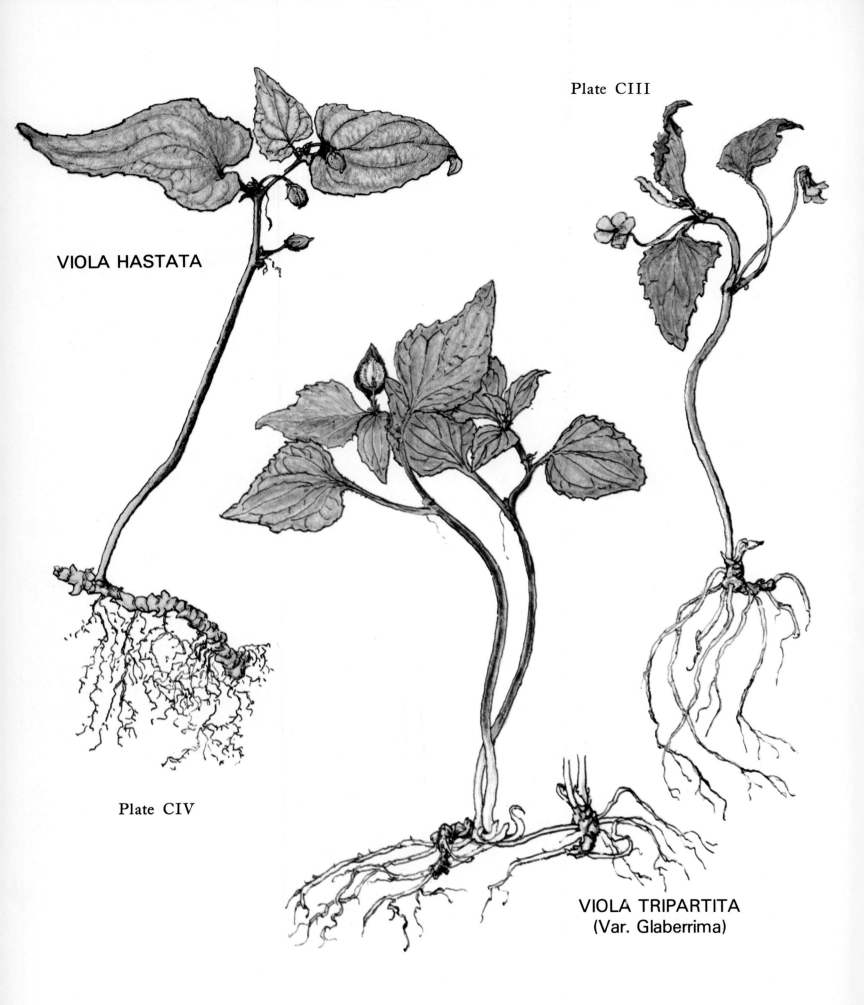

VIOLA HASTATA

Plate CIII

Plate CIV

VIOLA TRIPARTITA
(Var. Glaberrima)

174

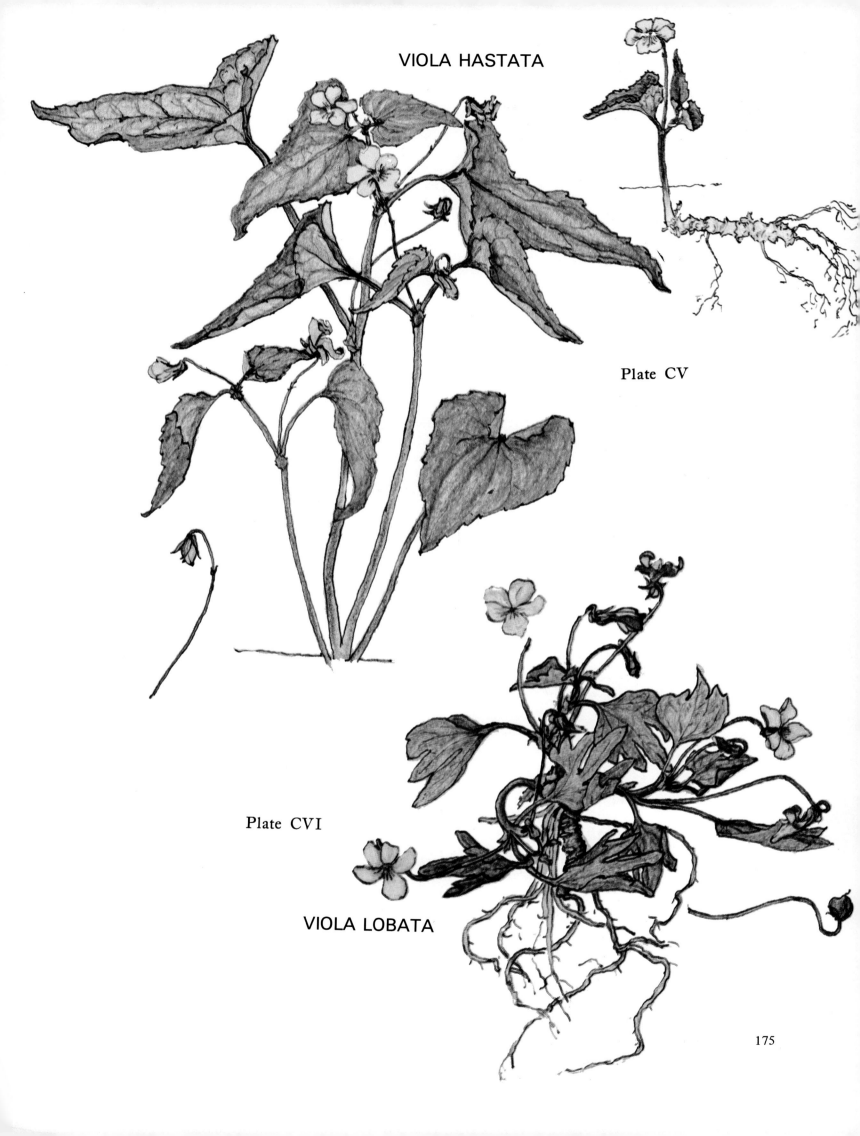

VIOLA HASTATA

Plate CV

Plate CVI

VIOLA LOBATA

175

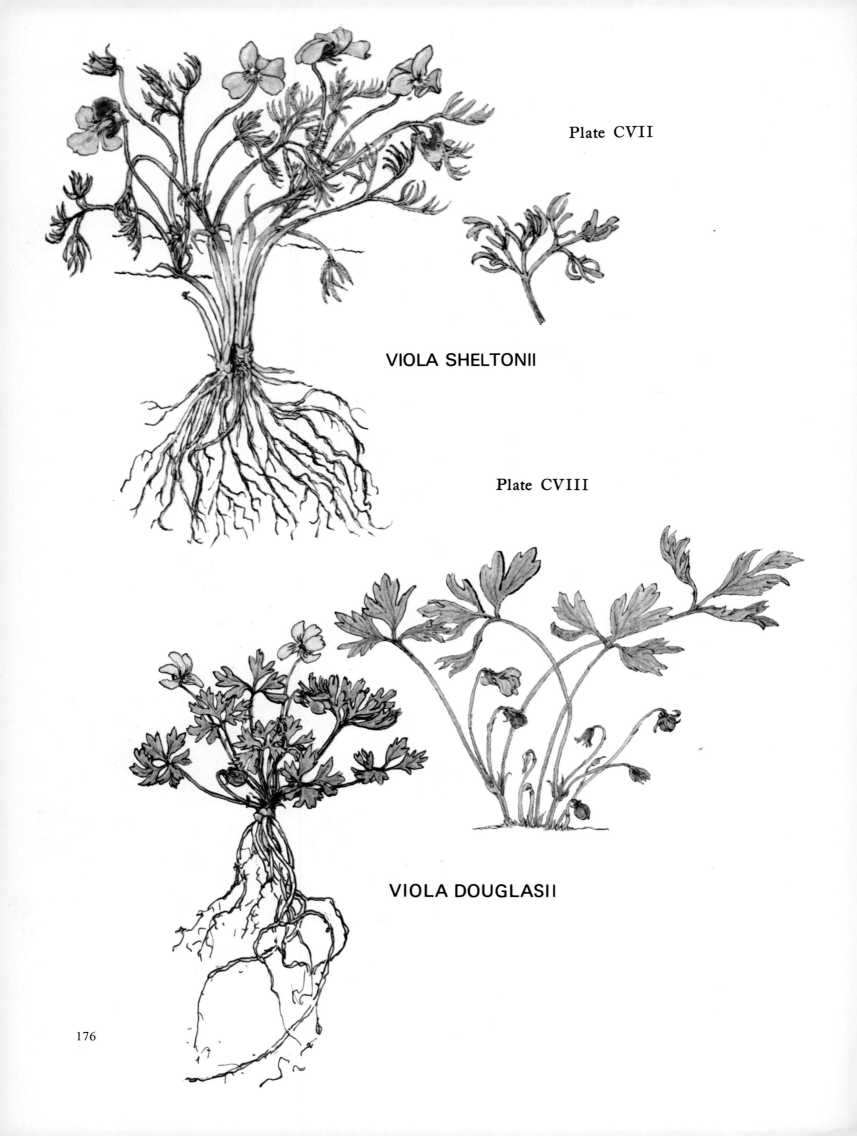

Plate CVII

VIOLA SHELTONII

Plate CVIII

VIOLA DOUGLASII

VIOLA RAFINESQUII Greene

Wild Pansy

Plate LXXXII

This delicate little plant is one of the two annual violets in the United States. It is widespread from Pennsylvania to the southwest and midwest and has been reported as far west as Colorado and Arizona.

A plant from Pennsylvania had white flowers with a tinge of blue, while the herbarium specimen from the University of Pennsylvania is colored a pale blue with white center, which is typical of those found farther west, according to Dr. Russell. Opal Flick from Indiana sent me some seeds with this comment: "I would advise planting it far away from any choice plants. It is a dainty thing when it first starts to bloom but keeps growing taller and with us is a weed, seeding all over."

The pectinate (comblike) stipules are characteristic of this violet as well as of *V. arvensis* and *V. tricolor*. The differences between the two annuals are: the leaves of *V. arvensis* are more deeply scalloped than those of *V. Rafinesquii,* which are almost entire; the sepals of the flowers are longer than the petals, the reverse of *V. Rafinesquii.* Also, *V. arvensis* is likely to be smaller flowered and yellow and white.

A moist, open, sandy (therefore well-drained) position would seem to fill its needs, though it has been reported in open woods too.

VIOLA ARVENSIS Murray

Wild Pansy

Plate LXXXIII

Viola arvensis is the other annual violet found in the United States. Those shown came from Ohio, a Pennsylvania herbarium specimen, and Texas. It was introduced from Europe but has naturalized in various parts of the country in fields and on roadsides, and can even be a weed in the south. In their youth both of these annuals look quite a bit like Johnny-Jump-Ups. Their common name indicates how close they appear.

The differences between the two annuals have been pointed out under *Viola Rafinesquii.*

If you can procure seeds of it, it should grow readily in sandy or well-drained soil. I thought it hardly strong enough to become a pest until I saw some herbarium sheets and realized how tall and rather coarse it can grow. You are warned!

GROUP VII

STEMLESS YELLOW
UNCUT

VIOLA ROTUNDIFOLIA Michx.

Round-leaved Violet

Plates LXXXIV, LXXXV

As this precious violet, *Viola rotundifolia,* is the only stemless yellow violet, it should not be difficult to recognize. However, other yellow violets that show manifest stems later, may in their early stages appear stemless. Its closest relative is *orbiculata* (Plate XCVI) of the west. The latter has smooth, firm leaves without the pubescence of *V. rotundifolia;* the rootstock is different, while the cleistogenes of *V. rotundifolia* are on racemelike branches.

Another western violet with which *V. rotundifolia* might be confused is *V. sempervirens* in its compact form, but the roots are different and the cleistogenes of *V. sempervirens* (Plate XCIV) have leaves on their branches. Also, the shape and color of the flowers differ.

Viola rotundifolia is an eastern plant, found roughly from New England to North Carolina. Those on Plate LXXXIV came from Pennsylvania and Vermont; those on Plate LXXXV from Connecticut. The leaves of *V. rotundifolia* become much larger with age, so that they are hardly recognizable as the same plant. They retain some pubescence and lie flat on the ground. The plant then produces its leafless prostrate racemes of purplish cleistogenes.

The clear-yellow, white-centered flowers have brownish striations on the lower petals and are held even with or just above the leaves.

Viola rotundifolia is found in cool, rich woods, beech or hemlock and hardwood forests, so that we must give it a shaded position in good soil on the acid side if we hope to cultivate it. Where suited it will make a groundcover.

GROUP VIII

STEMMED YELLOW
UNCUT

Violas Bakeri
        Nuttallii & vallicola
        praemorsa
        purpurea
        venosa
        pedunculata
        sempervirens
        orbiculata
        biflora
        pubescens eriocarpa
        pubescens
        glabella
        tripartita
        tripartita variety glaberrima
        hastata

VIOLA BAKERI Greene

VIOLA NUTTALLII var. BAKERI

Baker's Violet

Plates LXXXVI, XCII

While *Viola Bakeri* is considered a variety of *V. Nuttallii,* here again most gardeners would feel that it should be known by a specific name.

Viola Bakeri, as shown on plants from Oregon (Plate LXXXVI), has a deep seated rootstock branching at the top into persistent woody divisions, quite different from the *Nuttallii-vallicola* complex. The stem is not very evident, but a small part of it persists when the upper part dies down. A flowering stem is shown on Plate XCII next to *V. venosa.* The softly pubescent leaves may be toothed, as those illustrated on Plate LXXXVI, or they may be almost entire, as shown on Plate XCII, and then would appear nearer to the *Nuttallii* group. The flowers are pale yellow on both sides, not having the rust on the back as in *Nuttallii.*

The plant comes from open ground and blooms at three inches high soon after the snow melts. It is found in the Cascades, the Siskiyous, and into Eldorado County, California. It is not an easy plant to cultivate.

VIOLA NUTTALLII Pursh.

Nuttall's Violet

VIOLA VALLICOLA Nelson

VIOLA 'GOLD NUGGET,' V. VALLICOLA FORM

Valley Violet, Nuttall's Violet

Plate LXXXVII

These two midwestern violets and the rare doubled form of *V. vallicola* are shown adjacent to each other for easy comparison. They have so many similarities that most botanists have placed them under the species *V. Nuttallii,* calling *V. vallicola* a variety of it. But they have so many differences that gardeners and growers may think of them as separate species with quite different personalities.

The similarities are obvious, so let us note the differences. One is habitat. *V. vallicola* likes a rich, moist, well-drained soil in part shade, and is usually found in mountain valleys. *V. Nuttallii,* on the other hand, is a plant of the prairies enjoying hot, dry positions. The gumbo clay in which it grows may be lightened with sand and gravel. Evidently the clay holds moisture, for planted on my hot, gravelly hillside in full sun, *V. Nuttallii* promptly disappeared. Two, the root systems are different. *V. Nuttallii* has a branching taproot, plus other roots. *V. vallicola* has a bunch of more or less even roots. Three, the leaves of *V. Nuttallii* are slightly pubescent, more of a blue-green, narrow and pointed with some toothing. Those of *V. vallicola*

are a yellowish-green, more rounded at the ends and only wavy edged.

Both plants are heavy bloomers, and frequently have more and larger flowers than those shown on the specimens I drew. *V. Nuttallii,* left-hand on Plate LXXXVII, is a small-flowered form from Colorado. All the other plants illustrated are from South Dakota. The leaves may also grow taller and larger.

'Gold Nugget,' so named by Claude Barr, was given to him in the 1930s by a Mrs. Nelson who found it growing in Phillips County, Montana, near the Canadian border.

These plants and most of the information on habitat, as well as helpful criticism of my drawings, came from Mr. Barr, who has studied and knows the plants of South Dakota probably better than anyone else.

Both plants have persisted in my garden for several years at this writing. They disappear completely over the winter. Both have been grown in well-drained soil, kept moderately moist in half-shade, and have come up and bloomed, though not with the abandon they show in their homeland.

VIOLA VALLICOLA

VIOLA NUTTALLII

VIOLA PRAEMORSA Dougl.

Astoria Violet

Plates LXXXVIII, LXXXIX

Viola praemorsa is a particularly attractive western violet from Oregon and California. All the illustrations are of Oregon plants except the lower left drawing on Plate LXXXIX. This came from Montana State University. It was first found at Astoria, Oregon; hence its common name. Its soft, rather fleshy, furry leaves and clear yellow flowers, veined purple, bearded, with rusty-red on the back of the upper petals on a well-balanced plant, all make for great charm.

It is said that when it was discovered it was growing in sandy soil with its short rootstock praemorse, or cut-off, which prompted its Latin name. In early spring the plants appear stemless but later develop short stems.

If you will look back to Plate LXXXVII you will note marked resemblance between *V. vallicola* and *V. praemorsa*, in the color of the flowers, manner of growth and root system. Some botanists consider *V. praemorsa* to be a variety or subspecies of *V. Nuttallii* too, and it may well be. However, the furriness of *V. praemorsa*, its larger leaves at flowering time, and of course its geographical location, distinguish it for gardeners.

As for cultivation, it is found in heavy soils as well as sandy, and is accustomed to long dry summers. A well-drained position in a rock-garden or on the slope of a hill would be indicated. Most of these western plants need some protection from full hot summer sun when grown in the east.

VIOLA PURPUREA Kell.

Pine or Mountain Violet

Plate XC

Viola purpurea, from Oregon, represents a complex of western violets. There are varieties known as *pinetorum* and *aurea; V. venosa* is also considered a variety of *V. purpurea.*

I thought *V. purpurea* meant purple-flowered, but not so. The flowers are yellow with purple to rust on the backs of the upper petals and purple lines on the fronts. The bearded blossoms overtop the leaves on peduncles rising from the axils of the upper leaves; capsules are rounded and pubescent; there are many cleistogenes. The smaller plant, found on a roadside bank in Washington, had larger flowers with no purple on the backs; seedpods and some of the leaves are different. It might be a form or hybrid of *V. purpurea.* Such are the vagaries of violets!

Viola purpurea has a rather shallow rootstock with several stems rising from the crown, toothed stipules, rather broad and deeply cut toothing to the slightly pubescent leaves that are sub-cordate to cuneate at the base, extending into the petioles. There is sometimes a purplish cast to the plant.

The habitat is open, coniferous forests in dry gravelly soil, from Washington down to California, blooming April to June.

Variety *V. pinetorum* is more pubescent, and *V. purpurea* var. *aurea* is densely white pubescent and has pale sage-green leaves.

We follow this species with an illustration and description of *V. purpurea* var. *venosa.* All these violets are most attractive, but away from their home base they do not seem too easy to cultivate. They have, however, reappeared in spring in my garden in well-drained soil in part shade, and given time I might learn to grow them well!

VIOLA VENOSA Wats.

VIOLA PURPUREA, var. VENOSA

Mountain Violet

VIOLA BAKERI Greene

Plates XCI, XCII

Charles Thurman, who sent me *Viola venosa,* said that it and *V. trinervata* have much in common—one an alpine mountain species, the other from the desert—since both grow in fine clayey volcanic ash soil, about two inches deep over fractured rock, *V. venosa* in serpentine, *V. trinervata* in basalt. Both are accustomed to drying out after blooming, but their roots penetrate the fissures of the rock where there is enough moisture to support them, yet where there is perfect drainage.

Viola venosa is lightly pubescent. The leaves are rather broad in proportion to their length and can be either entire or broadly and coarsely dentate. The plant is found in the mountains of Washington and California, and as far east as Montana and Colorado. Those shown came from Washington with flower adapted from herbarium sheet, University of Washington.

There is a woody branching rootstock (somewhat like that of *V. Bakeri,* Plate LXXXVI, but quite different from *V. purpurea*) to which the plant dies down after seeding. The seedheads are very small.

The flowers have bright red to rust on the back of the upper petals. The whole plant, above ground, has great delicacy and charm.

V. venosa lived over the winter here; it came up but did not bloom. It was in half-shade in soil on the acid side and well-drained, but it is one of the difficult violets to cultivate, for the rootstock needs the dry curing it gets in its native haunts.

VIOLA PEDUNCULATA Torr. & Gray

Yellow Pansy, California
Golden Violet
Johnny-Jump-Up

Plate XCIII

This gorgeous violet with its large, rich golden flowers is the delight of California from San Francisco Bay to San Diego and inland almost to Arizona. It grows in full sun in clay loam meadows or grassy hillsides. The plant pictured was sent to me from Sebastopol, California, by Jean Ireland. She wrote: "They grow in wide clumps and are very deep-rooted. The tops fan out from a deep-seated crown making a large plant. When I was a child I roamed the Potrero Hillside in San Francisco and picked great fistfuls of *V. pedunculata* along with other flowers. Now there is nothing there but houses." The plants are so truly perennial that they grow and reappear for years and years, coloring the fields yellow when in bloom.

The oval, rather triangular, scalloped leaves extend into the petioles at their base. The whole plant is somewhat pubescent and feels soft to the touch, but except on the petioles, one needs a mag-

nifying glass to see the hairs. The petioles and leaves have some of the reddish-brown coloring found on the back of the flowers. The flowers are large and are held well above the foliage on long peduncles; much the showiest of the western yellow violets.

The stems below ground are very brittle, making the plants difficult to dig. The almost cormlike rootstock is covered with heavy roots, the older ones somewhat woody.

For the sake of clarity, I could not show the many blossoming, leafy stems that make a big, spreading clump. The beautiful flowers are prized for home decoration and are sold in the flower markets.

Local cultivation seems to have no difficulties, but the plants are not hardy outdoors in colder climates.

VIOLA SEMPERVIRENS Greene

V. SARMENTOSA Dougl.

Redwood Violet or Evergreen Violet

Plates XCIV, XCV

Though *Viola sempervirens* also grows farther north than the Redwoods, the common name does indicate that it is a woodland plant. It is found in both moist and dry positions and on woodland banks, mainly west of the Cascades in Washington and Oregon and on down into California. Dorothy Young wrote in *Wildflower Jewels,* "The Redwood Violet is a constant bloomer here in the warm area known as the banana belt on the southern Mendocino coast. The creeping plants make a carpet, yellow-starred, in company with calypso, vancouveria, Redwood-oxalis and ginger."

In addition to the small mountain forms (one from Oregon on Plate XCIV, one from Washington at the foot of Plate XCV) that somewhat resemble *V. orbiculata* (Plate XCVI, under which it is discussed further), it also forms much larger plants with larger, thinner, firm leaves, with long prostrate stems or stolons bearing leaves and flowers at intervals, making a plant that will cover a foot-wide space on the forest floor. The large plant on Plate XCV came from Jean Ireland, of Sebastopol, California, while the large-flowered drawing was adapted from a photograph.

The almost evergreen leaves are borne on reddish petioles, one to seven inches long. The stem-leaves as usual are smaller than the basal leaves. The clear lemon-yellow flowers with purple lines are bearded and arise from leaf-joints, usually held above the leaves. The capsules are oval, mottled purple. The closed flowers or. cleistogenes grow from the axils of the leaves. Blooming period in the northern habitats may extend from March to June.

Jean Ireland wrote me that she had success with the woodland form of *V. sempervirens* in a leafy, acid soil in shade, with moderate moisture, as it does not go dormant. The condensed mountain form would also need a peaty soil in half-shade in eastern gardens, with adequate but not excessive moisture.

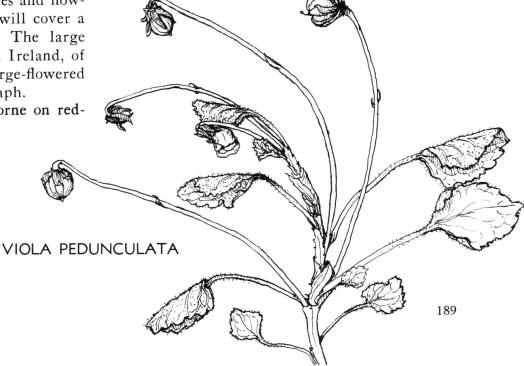

VIOLA PEDUNCULATA

189

VIOLA ORBICULATA Geyer

Western Round-leaved Violet

Plate XCVI

This little beauty is found in the northwest in deeply shaded, coniferous forest in Montana, Idaho, Oregon, and Washington—usually at high altitudes, 1500 to 3500 feet. My drawings were made from a slide from Oregon and plants from Montana and Washington. Although it is considered a close relative of the eastern *V. rotundifolia,* in the west it might be confused with the small mountain form of *V. sempervirens,* for they are both low-growing with yellow flowers. There are, however, a number of noticeable differences.

Viola sempervirens has fleshier leaves with perhaps a brownish tinge above and below; *V. orbiculata* has thin, firm leaves inclined to be somewhat concave, of a deep green, lighter on the reverse. *V. sempervirens* has stolons; *V. orbiculata* does not have them. The rootstock of *V. sempervirens* is slender, while that of *V. orbiculata* is somewhat heavier with many fibrous roots. The leaves of *V. sempervirens* are more noticeably scalloped and tend to be evergreen, while those of *V. orbiculata* are only finely crenate and deciduous. *V. orbiculata* is found at higher altitudes than is *V. sempervirens.*

The fall leaves of *V. orbiculata* are very noticeable in the dark woods because of their deep red color. The flowers are a rich lemon-yellow with purple veining; they grow lower than or just above the leaves, coming from the axils of the upper leaves on short pedicels, as do the cleistogenes, which keep on developing until the end of the season.

The culture for *V. orbiculata,* as for the woodland form of *V. sempervirens,* is to grow it in shady, acid-soil forest duff.

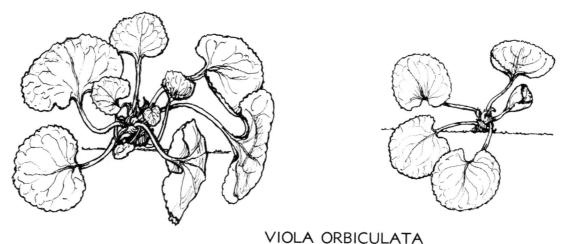

VIOLA ORBICULATA

VIOLA BIFLORA L.

Two-flowered Yellow Violet

Plate XCVII

Not having received any plants of *V. biflora* at the time, I drew the two large ones on Plate XCVII one from a colored photograph, one from a slide. You can imagine my surprise when I received three plants from Alaska and found both plants and flowers so small.

One plant was received from Christine Heller who said it was so little because it had just come up and that later they grow to be four to five inches high. She found it at low altitude near the roadside in a spot shaded by willows, but she said that they also grow in exposed places or on rocky ledges. Helen White sent me plants from just such a position—a steep bank of gravel which has natural seepage but was dry at the time. She said it was at an altitude of 3700 feet and that it was shaded by other plants but no trees.

You might momentarily confuse it with the yellow-flowered *V. orbiculata* but on examination you will find that the flowers are a different shape, the leaves of *V. orbiculata* much firmer but not so evenly scalloped as are those of *V. biflora,* the cleistogenes of *V. orbiculata* low and reddish, while *V. biflora*'s rise from the joints of the upper leaves and are green. In addition, *V. orbiculata* has a definite red bud at the center of the plant; *V. biflora* does not. Besides, *V. biflora* is noticeably stemmed, while *V. orbiculata* is not, though one can find a very small stem underground.

V. biflora is found in the mountains of Colorado as well as in Alaska. It is supposed to have migrated to this country from Europe and Siberia where it still grows. Other "old-world" violets, such as *V. Selkirkii* and *V. palustris,* are frequently found in the neighborhood of *V. biflora.* Such a widespread species must be able to adapt to varying conditions, which is true of many plants that have survived through the ages.

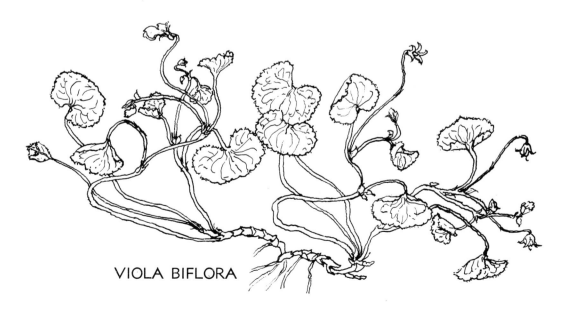

VIOLA BIFLORA

191

VIOLA PUBESCENS Ait.

Downy Yellow Violet

VIOLA PUBESCENS var. ERIOCARPA (Schwein.) Russell

Smooth Yellow Violet

VIOLA PUBESCENS var. INEXPECTA Wherry

Unexpected Violet

Plates XCVIII, XCIX

Even all these names do not cover this species, for *V. eriocarpa* has also been known as *V. Pensylvanica.*

This widespread species with its many variations is the cause of considerable disagreement among botanists of the "bunch" school and the "split" school. For our purposes I can do no better than to quote Dr. Russell's *Violets of Eastern and Central U.S.*: "The two varieties of *Viola pubescens,* as treated here, have long been considered separate . . . species by taxonomists. However, such students of the violets as Ezra Brainerd (1921) have noted their intergradation in nature and remarked upon the difficulty of distinguishing them. After studying several thousand specimens . . . I believe that only a single species exists . . ."

The main differences that Russell lists are: *V. pubescens* is usually very hairy, tall (to a foot or more), and grows in dry, shaded woods; *V. eriocarpa* is smooth or slightly hairy, lower (often six inches or less tall) and grows in open moist mead-

ows. They both start to bloom while very small.

Dr. Wherry found white-flowered plants growing among yellow ones in Pennsylvania and was surprised, as these yellow-flowered species rarely have white forms, so he called it *"inexpecta."* Although only one of the plants shown on Plate XCIX is hairy. Dr. Russell considers them all forms of *V. pubescens,* while the lower, leafier plant on Plate XCVIII is *Viola pubescens var. eriocarpa.*

One of the closest relatives of *V. pubescens* is *Viola glabella* of the Black Hills, South Dakota, and western mountains. We show it on Plates XCVIII and XCIX, and one can readily see how close it is. The plants start low, with a strong resemblance to *V. eriocarpa,* and grow taller as they go to seed, with marked resemblance then to *V. pubescens.* The root system is different, *V. glabella* having a running rhizome that emits plants at intervals.

VIOLA GLABELLA Nutt.

The Stream Violet

Plates C, CI

Viola glabella is found in moist, wooded areas from the western mountains to the Pacific coast and from Alaska to California. In this area it is perhaps the most common violet. The drawings on Plate C came from South Dakota plants; on Plate CI, the upper picture was adapted from a photograph, the lower ones were drawn from plants from Montana and Alaska.

V. glabella's horizontal rootstock is covered with scales and long, fibrous roots. There are two to three basal leaves, and a long stem at the top of which leaves and flowers are emitted. The leaves are round or kidney-shaped, scalloped, acute; the stem leaves smaller. The flowers are on short pedicels, deep lemon-yellow, purple-veined and bearded. The oblong green capsules are a different shape from those of *V. pubescens*. Cleistogenes grow from the axils of the upper leaves.

Viola glabella is considered a good plant for naturalizing in the woods (as is the *pubescens* group), where it will cover large areas. It is known to carpet the fir woods near Portland, Oregon, and grows under the Sequoias in a dwarf form. It is also reported as growing in the Black Hills in South Dakota.

VIOLA TRIPARTITA Ell.

Three-parted Violet

VIOLA TRIPARTITA var. GLABERRIMA Harper

Uncut var. of Tripartita

Plates CII, CIII

Viola tripartita has both a cut-leaved and an uncut form, *glaberrima* (Russell considers only one species present). I have placed it with the uncut yellow violets, since it has many similarities with the other long-stemmed yellows and it will be easier to compare when shown close to them. It is also mentioned under the cut-leaved forms to avoid confusion.

Viola tripartita, in its typical form, has deeply three-parted leaves. These, instead of being heart-shaped at the bottom, as in *Violas pubescens* and *glabella,* are cuneate and come to a point at the base. The same is true of *Viola glaberrima,* except that some of the leaves extend into the petiole.

The rather woody rootstock differs from the others in having running stolons that send up new plants at intervals. (In *V. glabella* a running root-stock does this.) The thong-like roots indicate that this violet comes from a moist position.

The plant of *V. tripartita* came from Pennsylvania; the plant of *V. glaberrima* from Marshall University in West Virginia. They are found throughout the southern Appalachians, into the Carolinas, Georgia and Tennessee. Usually, both forms are found growing together.

The flowers are comparatively small, yellow on both front and back, and grow from the axils of the leaves at the top of the stem. The pods on *V. glaberrima* are pubescent along the divisions. On *V. tripartita* the pods are smooth, but there is some slight pubescence on backs and edges of leaves and stipules.

There should be no difficulty in growing these violets.

VIOLA HASTATA Michx.

Halberd-leaved or Spear-leaved Violet

Plates CIV, CV

Although this violet might at a casual glance be mistaken for the *glaberrima* form of the preceding species, the heart-shape at the base of the leaves readily distinguishes it. Even more characteristic (though not so easily seen) is the deep-seated, horizontally creeping, white, brittle rootstock. This does look a great deal like the rootstock of *Viola glabella* from the west, its nearest relative. However, *Viola hastata* is an eastern species from mountain forests and dry woods from Pennsylvania to Ohio, the Appalachians to Florida. Both those shown came from Pennsylvania.

The halberd-shaped, toothed, patterned leaves on slender glabrous stems arise singly or in pairs along the rootstock, sometimes showing basal leaves, and with stem-leaves clustered near the top. The yellow flowers are tinged purple on the outside, are purple lined, and sparsely bearded. They grow on short pedicels from the axils of the upper leaves, which also emit cleistogamous flowers later in the season. The plant blooms in April and May and disappears entirely after seeding.

It can color a bank yellow, and given half-shade in woodland or other good soil, it can readily be cultivated.

GROUP IX

STEMMED YELLOW
CUT-LEAVED

Violas lobata
Sheltonii
Douglasii

Note: *V. tripartita,* which is also cut-leaved and yellow, was described in Group VIII, Plate CII.

VIOLA LOBATA Benth.

Yellow Wood Violet
Pine Violet

Plate CVI

Here is another of the interesting yellow violets from the Pacific Coast. This one came from Oregon. The leaves readily distinguish *Viola lobata* from all other violets by their deep, varied, irregular lobing and cuneate base. They grow near the top of the purplish stems and may be smooth or pubescent. There is a form of *V. lobata* called *V. l. integrifolia,* which has no lobing but has toothing on the upper half of the leaves.

The flowers are rust-colored on the back of the two upper petals and may have some of this color on the other petals too. The lines are brownish and the beards yellow. Cleistogamous flowers are borne in the axils of the upper leaves.

The rootstock is thick and fleshy with strong roots.

Viola lobata can be found in bloom from March to July in open, coniferous forests from Oregon to California, frequently on dry slopes.

It is an easier plant to cultivate than some of the other westerners, given forest duff or other rich, open, acid soil in part shade, in a well-drained area.

VIOLA SHELTONII Torr.

Shelton's Violet

Plate CVII

Viola Sheltonii is valued as much for its foliage as for its sparse, pale-yellow, narrow, delicate flowers that overtop it. It is a widespread westerner from Washington to California and in the Rockies of Montana and Colorado, flowering (depending on locality) from March to June. It is shown as received in early spring from Oregon, and also in bloom in my garden the following spring. It is usually found under pines or in thorny thickets called chaparral, on moist slopes, or if among rocks, in more open positions.

Its lovely, blue-green, dissected leaves, somewhat like some of the small delphiniums found in the same areas, are lighter below, with purplish veining that may give the back of the leaf a purple tone. The yellow, purple-veined, slightly bearded flowers, like so many of the other yellow violets, have rusty to purple tones on the back. Cleistogamous flowers rise from below soil level on long peduncles.

Albert Sutton wrote me from Washington, "I have had it in my garden but it never bloomed, which suited me fine as the mass of foliage is all the decoration you need." Boyd Kline says, "Give it lots of leafmold, gritty soil and a bit of shade."

VIOLA DOUGLASII Steudl.

V. CHRYSANTHA Hook

Golden Violet or Douglas Violet

Plate CVIII

Viola Douglasii is one of the most beautiful of the western violets, blooming early, appearing March to May. Like so many desert plants, *Viola Douglasii* has stems that are mostly subterranean, attached to a deep-seated rootstock with heavy roots, to which it dies down after seeding. It is found along the coast from Oregon to Southern California, in various types of soil. Near Medford, Oregon, from where this plant was received, it was reported by Boyd Kline as growing in clay soil among pot-holes filled with water in winter and spring and dust-dry in summer. Elsewhere it has been found on grassy slopes and on dry, open slopes in gravelly soil.

The stems above soil level are purple and bear finely slashed leaves on long petioles. The large, golden flowers overtop the leaves, are veined dark with yellow beards, and have dark rust to almost black on the back of the upper petals. The plant has green capsules but no cleistogenes.

As you will note, it is a plant that grows in well-drained to desert conditions, which makes it difficult to cultivate in the east or any part of the country that has a heavy rainfall. A rock-garden with no artificial watering in summer would seem to be the only hope of having it survive.

APPENDIX

Nurseries

Most nurseries have wild violets for sale. Here are a few that have some of the more unusual ones:

Orchid Gardens, Route 1, Box 441, Grand Rapids, Minnesota 55744

Prairie Gem Ranch (Claude A. Barr), Smithwick, South Dakota 57782

Siskiyou Rare Plant Nursery (Crocker & Kline), 522 Franquette Street, Medford, Oregon 97501

The Three Laurels, Marshall, North Carolina 28753

The Wild Garden (George Schenk), Box 487 Bothell, Washington 98011

Most nurseries have lists; a nursery with a large catalog may charge for it, but will usually refund the money with the first order.

Violet seeds can sometimes be obtained through seed exchanges by members of the following societies:

American Rock Garden Society
American Primrose Society

Geographical Distribution

These lists represent the areas from which I have received the various species, but most violets have a way of spreading beyond their so-called boundaries. Frequently, where they meet other species they hybridize with them or "intergrade." On the whole, though, this approximation is a reasonably good guide as to where you might find the various species. You will find some on more than one list.

East & West
adunca
canadensis
nephrophylla
odorata

East
affinis
appalachiensis
arvensis
blanda
Brittoniana
canadensis
conspersa
cucullata
eriocarpa
fimbriatula
hastata
hirsutula
incognita
lanceolata
novae-angliae
odorata
pallens (Macloskeyi
    pallens)
palmata
pedata
primulifolia
pubescens
Rafinesquii
rostrata
rotundifolia
sagittata
septemloba
septentrionalis
sororia
striata
tricolor
triloba

Midwest
glabella
missouriensis
montanensis
nuttallii
pedatifida

pratincola
pubescens
Rafinesquii
rugulosa
sororia
vallicola
viarum

West
Bakeri
Beckwithii
cuneata
Douglasii
Flettii
glabella
Hallii
Howellii
lobata
Macloskeyi
occidentalis
ocellata
odorata
pedunculata
praemorsa
purpurea
sempervirens
Sheltonii
trinervata
venosa

South
Egglestonii
esculenta
floridana
glaberrima
hirsutula
kauaiensis (from
    Hawaii)
Langloisii
Lovelliana
odorata
pedata
primulifolia
septemloba
trachellifolia
    (from Hawaii)

tripartita
villosa
vittata (lanceolata
    vittata)
Walteri

North
biflora
epipsela
labradorica
Langsdorfii
nephrophylla
palustris
renifolia
Selkirkii

Positions Found

These lists are a rough guide. Most violets will grow anywhere and you sometimes wish they wouldn't. A few, such as *V. pedata,* need acid soil. Think of the weedy violets as lovely groundcovers, and cosset the difficult ones to have the pleasure of their company.

Some violets will be found on more than one list.

Violets for Sun
adunca
arvensis
Beckwithii
conspersa
cucullata
cuneata
Douglasii
Egglestonii
eriocarpa
esculenta
floridana
Hallii
Howellii
kauiensis
Langloisii
missouriensis
montanensis
novae-angliae
Nuttalli
palmata
pedata
pedatifida
pedunculata
praemorsa
pratincola

primulifolia
Rafinesquii
septentrionalis
Sheltonii
sororia
trachellifolia
tricolor
vallicola
viarum
villosa

Violets for Moist Places
blanda
Brittoniana
cucullata
cuneata
epipsela
eriocarpa
esculenta
hastata
incognita
lanceolata
lanceolata vittata
Macloskeyii
missouriensis
nephrophylla

novae-angliae
occidentalis
orbiculata
pallens
palustris
pratincola (or dry)
primulifolia

Violets for Shade
adunca
affinis
appalachiensis
Bakeri
biflora
canadensis
conspersa
cuneata
fimbriatula
Flettii
glabella
glaberrima
hastata
hirsutula
incognita
inexpecta
labradorica

Langloisii
lobata
Lovelliana
missouriensis
nephrophylla
ocellata
orbiculata
odorata
pallens
palmata

pedata
pubescens
purpurea
renifolia
rostrata
rotundifolia
rugulosa
saggittata
Selkirkii
sempervirens

septemloba
septentrionalis
sororia
striata
triloba
tripartita
venosa
viarum
Walteri

BIBLIOGRAPHY

Abrams, Leroy. "Violets" in *Illustrated Flora of the Pacific States*. Stanford, California: Stanford University Press, 1960.

Bailey, Liberty Hyde. "Violets" in *The Standard Cyclopedia of Horticulture*. New York: Macmillan, 1922.

Brainerd, Ezra. *Violets of North America* (bulletin). Vermont Agricultural Experiment Station, 1921. (Out of print.)

Farrer, Reginald. *The English Rock Garden*. London: T. C. & E. C. Jack Ltd., 1925.

Gabrielson, Ira N. *Western American Alpines*. New York: Macmillan, 1932.

Gray, Asa. *Manual of Botany.* New York: American Book Company, 1908.

Heller, Christine. *Wild Flowers of Alaska*. Portland, Oregon: Graphic Arts Center, 1966.

Hitchcock, C. Leo and others, eds. "Violets" in *Vascular Plants of the Pacific Northwest*. Seattle, Washington: University of Washington, 1961.

Russell, Norman H. *Violets of the Central and Eastern United States* (bulletin). Dallas, Texas: Sida (Lloyd H. Shinners) (private publisher), 1965.

Schenk, George. *Rock Gardens*. Menlo Park, California: Lane Book Company, 1964.

Strausbaugh, P. D. & Core, E. A. *Flora of West Virginia* (bulletin). West Virginia University, 1958.

Wherry, Edgar T. *Violet Bulletin*. Pennsylvania: Bucks County Park Board, 1965.

Young, Dorothy K. *Wildflower Jewels*. Healdsburg, California: Naturegraph Publishers, 1964.

INDEX

INDEX OF COMMON NAMES